The *Hope Recovery* Devotional

There Is Always Hope With God

Greg Schmalhofer

Published by Greg Schmalhofer
ISBN-13 978-0-578-33619-0

Cover photo and design courtesy of Canva.com and Pexels.com.

Dedication

The Hope Recovery Devotional is dedicated to all of our dear friends at the faith-based Discovery Recovery group. We are blessed beyond measure to be a part of this group.

The Hope Recovery Devotional

There Is Always Hope With God

Introduction

The Hope Recovery Devotional is a 100 day devotional to help you be successful in recovery and to help you grow in your faith. Regardless of where you are in your recovery, whether you are at one day, one year, or many years, this devotional shares the powerful message that *there is always hope with God* and that you can indeed be successful in recovery. Each day includes a Scripture passage, inspirational message, brief prayer, and space to make journal entries along these 100 days. This devotional may be read as a daily devotional, or as part of a "90 meetings in 90 days" jumpstart, or any way to help you be successful in recovery. I suggest you consider a reading plan or schedule for when you will read this devotional, perhaps each day in the quiet of the morning or in the evening towards the end of the day. There are many recovery and faith principles presented throughout the devotional, but most reflect the key principle there is always hope with God. As you read *The Hope Recovery Devotional,* consider for yourself there truly is hope with God and with God in your life you can be successful in recovery and even over any struggle of life.

The Twelve Steps of Recovery from both *Alcoholics Anonymous* and *Narcotics Anonymous* have helped many millions of people be successful in recovery and one of the key principles of the Twelve Steps of Recovery is a spiritual experience with God. *The Hope Recovery Devotional* references the Twelve Steps of Recovery and the importance of a spiritual experience with God. In addition, this devotional presents what I call the Twelve Keys of Faith-Based Recovery, which takes a deeper look at recovery and this spiritual experience with God. The *Alcoholics Anonymous* and *Narcotics Anonymous* Twelve Steps of Recovery and the Twelve Keys of Faith-Based recovery are each listed after this introduction to prepare you for the devotional and for quick reference later. Regardless of where you are at with God today, I encourage you to be open to the possibility of having a spiritual experience with God.

The Hope Recovery Devotional is intended for individuals in recovery from alcohol or drugs, but it is appropriate for individuals struggling with any addictive behavior and even for anyone seeking to refresh their faith. It is my hope and prayer that this devotional will help you be successful in recovery and also help you grow in your faith. I encourage you to make the commitment to do whatever is necessary to be successful in recovery and to embrace the message *there is always hope with God.*

The Twelve Steps of Alcoholics Anonymous

1. We admitted we were powerless over alcohol—that our lives had become unmanageable.
2. Came to believe that a Power greater than ourselves could restore us to sanity.
3. Made a decision to turn our will and our lives over to the care of God *as we understood Him.*
4. Made a searching and fearless moral inventory of ourselves.
5. Admitted to God, to ourselves, and to another human being the exact nature of our wrongs.
6. Were entirely ready to have God remove all these defects of character.
7. Humbly asked Him to remove our shortcomings.
8. Made a list of all persons we had harmed, and became willing to make amends to them all.
9. Made direct amends to such people wherever possible, except when to do so would injure them or others.
10. Continued to take personal inventory and when we were wrong promptly admitted it.
11. Sought through prayer and meditation to improve our conscious contact with God *as we understood Him*, praying only for knowledge of His will for us and the power to carry that out.
12. Having had a spiritual awakening as the result of these steps, we tried to carry this message to alcoholics, and to practice these principles in all our affairs.

The Twelve Steps of Narcotics Anonymous

1. We admitted that we were powerless over our addiction, that our lives had become unmanageable.
2. We came to believe that a Power greater than ourselves could restore us to sanity.
3. We made a decision to turn our will and our lives over to the care of God as we understood Him.
4. We made a searching and fearless moral inventory of ourselves.
5. We admitted to God, to ourselves, and to another human being the exact nature of our wrongs.
6. We were entirely ready to have God remove all these defects of character.
7. We humbly asked Him to remove our shortcomings.
8. We made a list of all persons we had harmed, and became willing to make amends to them all.
9. We made direct amends to such people wherever possible, except when to do so would injure them or others.
10. We continued to take personal inventory and when we were wrong promptly admitted it.
11. We sought through prayer and meditation to improve our conscious contact with God as we understood Him, praying only for knowledge of His will for us and the power to carry that out.
12. Having had a spiritual awakening as a result of these steps, we tried to carry this message to addicts, and to practice these principles in all our affairs.

The Twelve Keys of Faith-Based Recovery (1-6)

1) There is a God in heaven.

- Psalm 46:10 *"Be still, and know that I am God."*
- There is a God in heaven; and he is a loving, caring, and compassionate God who wants to help you.

2) There is always hope with God.

- Isaiah 41:10 *"Fear not, for I am with you; Be not dismayed, for I am your God. I will strengthen you, Yes, I will help you." (NKJV)*
- With God there is always hope. You are not alone, God is with you and he wants to help you.

3) Do you want to get well?

- John 5:6 *"When Jesus saw him lying there and learned that he had been in this condition for a long time, he asked him, 'Do you want to get well?'"*
- Do you want to get well and are you willing to do whatever is necessary to be successful in recovery?

4) Recovery is possible with God.

- Philippians 4:13 *"I can do all things through Christ who strengthens me." (NKJV)*
- Don't let you past dictate your future. With God recovery is absolutely possible.

5) God wants to forgive you.

- Psalm 103:10-12 *"He does not deal with us according to our sins.... [11] For as high as the heavens are above the earth, so great is his steadfast love toward those who fear him;[12] as far as the east is from the west, so far does he remove our transgressions from us.(ESV)*
- Regardless of what you have done in the past, God wants to forgive you!

6) Seek God and you will find him.

- Jeremiah 29:13 *"You will seek me and find me when you seek me with all your heart."*
- Seek God with all of your heart and you will find him.

The Twelve Keys of Faith-Based Recovery (7-12)

7) Jesus is the true Higher Power.

- *John 14:6 "Jesus answered, "I am the way and the truth and the life. No one comes to the Father except through me."*
- Jesus is the way, the truth, and the life and Jesus is the true Higher Power.

8) Make a decision to put your faith in Jesus.

- *John 3:16 "For God so loved the world that he gave his one and only Son, that whoever believes in him shall not perish but have eternal life."*
- Put your faith and trust in Jesus as the true Higher Power.

9) Surround yourself with like-minded people.

- *1 Corinthians 15:33 "Do not be misled: "Bad company corrupts good character."*
- Surround yourself with like-minded people that share your desire to be clean and sober and share your love for God.

10) God made you and called you for a purpose.

- *Jeremiah 29:11 "'For I know the plans I have for you,' declares the Lord, 'plans to prosper you and not to harm you, plans to give you hope and a future.'"*
- God has made you for a purpose; consider what has God called you to do?

11) Peace that surpasses all understanding.

- *Philippians 4:7 "And the peace of God, which surpasses all understanding, will guard your hearts and your minds in Christ Jesus." (ESV)*
- You will still have struggles, but with God in your life you can have 'a peace that surpasses all understanding'.

12) Continue to trust God no matter what.

- *Proverbs 3:5-6 "Trust in the Lord with all your heart; do not depend on your own understanding. [6] Seek his will in all you do, and he will show you which path to take."(NLT)*
- No matter what happens continue to put your faith and trust in God and he will give you guidance and wisdom.

Day 1 of 100

There Is a God in Heaven

Be still, and know that I am God.
(Psalm 46:10 ESV)

As you begin this 100 day recovery devotional, you may feel overwhelmed as you face your recovery with all the different situations, struggles, fears, changes, and all the decisions to be made for your recovery. You may feel you are all alone and that the challenge of recovery seems so difficult you are not sure you can make it. But you do not have to go through it alone. It is easy to forget or to lose sight of the simple truth there is a God in heaven. Yes, there is a God and even more than that, he is a loving, caring, and compassionate God who wants to help you. He wants to help you in your recovery and with all your challenges of life. You are not alone; God is with you and he wants to help you.

The passage today from Psalm 46 reminds us to "Be still", not just slow down, but to pause right amid the uncertainties of our recovery and to be reminded there is a God and he wants to help us. This passage instructs us to focus on God instead of our problems or circumstances. We are instructed to have confidence and to "know that I am God." *Alcoholics Anonymous* speaks to the importance of this passage and to this power when it states:

> "All I can say is that it's a Power greater than myself. If pressed, all I can do is follow the psalmist who said it long before me: '*Be still,* and know that I am God.'"[1]

Perhaps it has been quite a long time since you thought of God or a long time since you last said a prayer, but I encourage you today to embrace this great truth and this great instruction to "Be still, and know that I am God." Regardless of the many questions, fears, and uncertainties you might be facing I ask you to pause right now in your day, take a deep breath, and focus on God. Be reminded of the great truth: there is a God and he is a loving, caring, and compassionate

God and he wants to help you. You are not alone. As you embrace this truth, it really changes everything. Hold fast to this great truth about God and to know that you can have confidence there is a God and with God, there is always hope. You can be successful in recovery. It will not be quick or easy, but as you stay focused on God and take each day one day at a time, God will help you and you will see that recovery is possible; there is indeed a God in heaven and he wants to help you.

Prayer for today:

Dear Lord, thank you that you are with me and that I am not alone. Help me to cling fast to this great truth and for me to be still and focus on you.

Notes of gratitude, progress, concerns, and prayers for today:

____

____

____

____

____

____

____

____

____

____

Day 2 of 100

There Is Always Hope with God

Fear not, for I am with you; Be not dismayed, for I am your God. I will strengthen you, Yes, I will help you. (Isaiah 41:10 NKJV)

In the early days of your recovery, you may feel as though things are racing all around you out of control as you experience many thoughts and emotions that you have not felt in quite some time. As you consider your addiction, and all the past events of your life that have led you to this point today, you may feel discouraged, depressed, and fearful as you take these initial steps in recovery. You may feel it is not possible for you to make it in recovery, that it is possible for others, but not for you. In your own power and in your own strength, it is not possible. However, with God in your life, there is always hope. *Alcoholics Anonymous* addresses this newfound outlook on hope as:

> "My physical being has certainly undergone a transformation, but the major transformation has been spiritual. The hopelessness has been replaced by abundant hope and sincere faith."[2]

The passage today from Isaiah shares a great declaration and a great truth of Scripture that no matter what you are facing today and regardless of your personal circumstances this passage tells you to "Fear not" and to "Be not dismayed" because "I am with you...for I am your God." You are not alone and you are not without hope. As you bring God into your life and as you put your hope and trust in God, you can have confidence that God "will strengthen you" and even that God himself "will help you". What a great expression of hope with the words "Yes, I will help you." Today, you can have confidence in this passage and you can have confidence that God will indeed help you. Embrace this great truth that God is with you and that God will help you and will strengthen you. Hold fast to the truth, there is always hope with God because he has promised he will help you. Give yourself time to heal, continue to do the next right thing, and continue to bring God into your life. As you bring God into your life, you will see more and more clearly there is always hope with God.

Prayer for today:

Dear Lord, I thank you for your promises that you will be with me and that you will help me. Help me to cling to these promises and to never forget there is always hope with you.

Notes of gratitude, progress, concerns, and prayers for today:

____

____

____

____

____

____

____

____

____

____

Day 3 of 100

Do You Want to Get Well?

When Jesus saw him lying there and learned that he had been in this condition for a long time, he asked him, "Do you want to get well?" (John 5:6 NIV)

Despite the wreckage and damage of your past, you have the opportunity to change the direction of your life. Today, and even every day, you can decide to do everything necessary to be successful in recovery. Perhaps you have tried recovery many times before and failed, but today you can make the commitment to do everything necessary to be successful in recovery. Be open to the idea of seeking God and to bringing God into your life. Recovery and bringing God into your life may seem vague and uncertain, but let me suggest it all begins with how you answer one very important question. "Do you want to get well?"

Jesus asked this question to a man who had been in bondage to his disabled physical condition for 38 years. Perhaps you feel you have been in bondage to drugs and alcohol for many years and maybe even decades. But the fact you are reading this book right now indicates how you have answered this question; yes, you want to get well! Certainly, right now you don't know what your recovery story will be, but you can be confident that God will help you every day and even every moment.

Jesus saw the man lying there trapped in his physical bondage and Jesus had compassion on him and asked him the simple question, "Do you want to get well?" Today, God sees you and your bondage to drugs and alcohol and God has compassion for you and wants to help you in your recovery. God wants to help you get well just as he helped this man in this passage. Jesus did not tell him all the details of how he would be made well, but just the simple question, "Do you want to get well?" For you today, God does not want you to be overwhelmed with all the details of your recovery; God just wants you to answer the simple question, "Do you want to get well?" God knows what you need for your recovery and to be made well, and he simply wants you to trust him. For today, embrace the decision you have made to get well and that you are willing to do whatever is necessary to be successful in recovery. Then continue to trust God as he leads you on your road of recovery and as he guides you in just the right steps for you to be made well.

Prayer for today:

Dear Lord I do want to get well. Please give me the wisdom and courage to follow your leading and to stay true to my commitment to do everything necessary to be successful in recovery.

Notes of gratitude, progress, concerns, and prayers for today:

____

____

____

____

____

____

____

____

____

____

Day 4 of 100

A Very Different Life

The thief comes only to steal and kill and destroy; I have come that they may have life, and have it to the full. (John 10:10 NIV)

As you start on your road of recovery, you may dwell on your past life in addiction and remember all the terrible pain you experienced and the pain you caused others. You may feel your past life left you broken and damaged in so many ways you have many doubts you can ever be successful in recovery. You may feel you are beyond hope. But the message of the Bible is clear: there is always hope with God. Certainly, the life of addiction will only lead to destruction, but God wants something very different for you. God wants you to have a full and abundant life. A full and abundant life is possible, but it starts by first putting your hope in God.

By putting your hope in God and embracing this life-changing commitment to do everything necessary to be successful in recovery, you recognize there absolutely needs to be change in your life. You cannot do the same things you've done in the past; rather, you need to make dramatic changes, consistent with the recovery principle 'if nothing changes, then nothing changes'. This does not happen all at once, but it starts by changing your focus and putting your hope in God. This passage from the Gospel of John is consistent with Step One of *Narcotics Anonymous,* that states: "We admitted that we were powerless over our addiction, that our lives had become unmanageable."[3]

As you reflect on your past life, you will likely see "the thief" of addiction was taking you in a direction that would end in destruction and possibly death. Jesus tells us in this passage he desires something very different for us and for you. Jesus came that you might have life, true life, and a life that is full and abundant. Right now, that might not seem possible today, but I encourage you to continue to trust God and continue to put your hope in God. Even though you may not understand what that actually looks like, continue to cling to the commitment to do everything necessary to be successful in recovery and continue to put your hope in God. Don't seek details of tomorrow, or next week, or next month, just focus on today. Embrace today, embrace your recovery, and as you continue to put your hope and trust in God, he will lead you on a path to a very different life, a full and abundant life.

Prayer for today:

Dear Lord, thank you for the promise of a full and abundant life. I do not yet understand how that will happen, but I do trust you to guide me every day in the needed changes and I look forward to a very different life even starting today.

Notes of gratitude, progress, concerns, and prayers for today:

____

____

____

____

____

____

____

____

____

____

Day 5 of 100

Recovery Is Possible with God

I can do all things through Christ who strengthens me. (Philippians 4:13 NKJV)

Recovery is not easy. It may be the most difficult challenge of your entire life. But it is absolutely possible with God in your life. As you continue with the life-changing decision to do everything necessary to be successful in recovery and your willingness to bring God into your life, I encourage you to not limit what God can do. In your own strength and in your own power, it is not possible, but with God in your life, recovery is absolutely possible. Allow the power of God to move in your life.

Many people are successful in recovery because of what God has done in their life; do not limit God and what he can do in your life. It is also important to not let your past define your future. Leave your past in the past. With God in your life, your future can be dramatically different from your past. *Alcoholics Anonymous* echoes this point with:

> "Our whole attitude and outlook upon life will change....We will suddenly realize that God is doing for us what we could not do for ourselves."[4]

Give God full access and control of all aspects of your life and your recovery and your attitude and outlook on life will change as well.

In this passage in Philippians, the apostle Paul instructs us to look to the strength that comes through Christ. God will help us and he will give us the strength and power to be successful in recovery and our entire outlook on life will gradually change. As you continue on in your recovery, continue to look to the strength and power that only God can provide. Embrace the truth of this passage that recovery is not easy, but that you can "do all things through Christ who strengthens" you and that includes being successful in recovery.

Continue on step by step and one day at a time and remember recovery is absolutely possible with God in your life.

Prayer for today:

Dear Lord, help me to leave the past in the past and to focus on you. Thank you that with your strength and power recovery is absolutely possible.

Notes of gratitude, progress, concerns, and prayers for today:

____

____

____

____

____

____

____

____

____

____

Day 6 of 100

You Have Another Chance

Jesus said, "Did I not tell you that if you believe, you will see the glory of God?" [43] When he had said this, Jesus called in a loud voice, "Lazarus, come out!" [44] The dead man came out....Jesus said to them, "Take off the grave clothes and let him go.
(John 11:40-44 NIV)

Many have died from the devastation of drugs and alcohol. Perhaps you were near death from an overdose and had to have an emergency treatment of naloxone (NARCAN) to bring you back. Some individuals have even been revived multiple times from multiple overdose incidents. Unfortunately, there are many that tragically died from drugs and alcohol. But if you are reading this book, that means you are not dead. Drugs and alcohol did not kill you. You have another chance. You have another opportunity to be successful in recovery and you have another opportunity to trust God with your life.

In this passage, the apostle John describes how Jesus brought Lazarus back to life again in dramatic fashion. Lazarus had been dead for four days and for Jesus to bring him back to life was a dramatic demonstration of the power of God when all else failed. You may feel that you were almost dead the way you were living your life in the past. While Jesus is no longer with us physically here on earth, the very same power of God is still available. God still says to us and to you today that "if you believe, you will see the glory of God." Embrace this tremendous power of God and believe God to move in your life. You have another chance! You have another opportunity to see the power of God and the glory of God in your life. Take off the "grave clothes" of your past life and go now with God. You have another chance, a second chance at life. I encourage you to make the most of this brand new opportunity; God has saved you for a reason. Bring God into your life and trust him and you will see the power of

God and the glory of God in your life and you will begin to see you do indeed have another chance at life.

Prayer for today:

Dear Lord, thank you that I am not dead, but that I am alive and have another chance at life. Help me to honor you with this new opportunity at life starting even this very day.

Notes of gratitude, progress, concerns, and prayers for today:

____

____

____

____

____

____

____

____

____

____

Day 7 of 100

Accept Spiritual Healing

"Is it easier to say to the paralyzed man 'Your sins are forgiven,' or 'Stand up, pick up your mat, and walk?'" [10] ....Then Jesus turned to the paralyzed man and said, [11] "Stand up, pick up your mat, and go home!" [12] And the man jumped up, grabbed his mat, and walked out through the stunned onlookers. They were all amazed and praised God. (Mark 2:9-12 NLT)

The battle to be successful in recovery over drugs and alcohol is likely the most difficult battle you will ever face. It is a life or death battle. The physical dependence on drugs or alcohol may have started small and inconsequential, but over time it has become all consuming, taking up seemingly every waking hour. It is a physical battle unlike any other you have ever faced. However, the battle over addiction is not only a physical battle. It is also a spiritual battle. Perhaps you have been distant from God; perhaps you rejected God entirely, or maybe even hated God for various events in your life. Regardless of your feelings about God, your battle over drugs and alcohol is absolutely a physical battle, and it is also a spiritual battle. It is important to do everything possible to address the physical battle and also the spiritual battle.

God made us as both physical and spiritual beings and it is important to seek both physical and spiritual healing. Often, we focus only on the physical aspects of recovery and either minimize the spiritual side or, worse, not even consider the spiritual side of our recovery.

This passage from the apostle Mark tells how Jesus addresses both the physical healing of the paralyzed man by saying "pick up you mat, and walk" and also the spiritual aspect of the man in need of healing saying "Your sins are forgiven". It is important to do everything possible to be successful in recovery, and that includes both physical healing and spiritual healing. Wherever you are at with your understanding of God, I encourage you to seek to find God. He will reveal himself to you and he wants to forgive you just as Jesus forgave the sins of the man in this passage. Even today Jesus says to you "your sins are forgiven". Accept God's forgiveness. Seek to bring God into your life, even if you have no idea what this 'God thing is all about'. I encourage you to simply seek to find God and he will reveal himself to you. Accept the spiritual healing only God can provide. As you bring God into your life and accept his spiritual healing, you will be "amazed" at what God can do in your life.

Prayer for today:

Dear Lord, please help me to make wise decisions for my physical and spiritual healing. I humbly and gratefully accept the forgiveness you graciously offer even to me.

Notes of gratitude, progress, concerns, and prayers for today:

____

____

____

____

____

____

____

____

____

____

Day 8 of 100

Sick People Made Well

Now when Jesus heard this, he withdrew from there in a boat to a desolate place by himself. But when the crowds heard it, they followed him on foot from the towns.* [14] *When he went ashore he saw a great crowd, and he had compassion on them and healed their sick.

(Matt 14:13-14 ESV)

Several years ago, I attended a funeral service for a young man who had died from a drug overdose. At the service there was an open sharing time and a friend of the deceased shared how he was a long-time friend and had partied with the deceased man many times and he was now one of very few left of their group of friends. This young man commented that people in addiction are not bad people trying to become good, rather they are sick people trying to become well. This young man was beginning to understand his condition and the type of battle he faced. Recovery is more than just stopping the use of drugs and alcohol. Recovery is a transformation, a healing of the body, mind, and spirit. A healing, that with God in your life, you are made fully well.

This passage from the book of Matthew reveals again how Jesus saw a great crowd of people, people in need, with burdens and struggles. Jesus not only saw them, but he had compassion on them and then healed them as well. Today, Jesus sees you and has compassion for you. Jesus wants to meet your great need, and he wants to heal you. Your body needs physical healing and time to recover from many years of addiction and alcohol abuse, but also you need spiritual healing. Both physical and spiritual healing will take time. But, just as the crowds "followed him" you need to seek God and to bring God into your life and follow him as he directs you. God sees your great need, and he wants to meet it in a mighty way. Give yourself time to heal physically and spiritually. It takes time. There are no shortcuts. Be patient with yourself and your loved ones, but be diligent and consistent. Go to AA and NA meetings, go to faith-based meetings, go to church. Continue to seek God and he will reveal himself to you and he will have compassion on you and he will make you well. Take whatever steps are necessary to heal physically and spiritually and let God make you well.

Prayer for today:

Dear Lord, thank you that you see my great need for healing and I ask you to help me to be made fully well. Be with me day by day and help me to do everything necessary to be successful in recovery.

Notes of gratitude, progress, concerns, and prayers for today:

____

____

____

____

____

____

____

____

____

____

Day 9 of 100

God Wants to Forgive You

He does not deal with us according to our sins....
[11] For as high as the heavens are above the earth,
so great is his steadfast love toward those who fear him;
[12] as far as the east is from the west, so far does he remove our transgressions from us.
(Psalm 103:10-12 ESV)

Many that have been in addiction for years and even decades often feel they have lived such a terrible life that they cannot be forgiven by their loved ones and certainly not by God. Many in addiction want to recover but, they believe they have hurt too many people, caused too much damage, destroyed too many relationships, and have rejected God so often that they think it is too late for them. They think they are too "bad" for God to forgive them.

Perhaps that is how you feel right now; that you have done too much against God for him to forgive you. Fortunately, this passage in Psalms tells us a different story, one of God's great mercy and compassion. The primary message of the Bible is that God is a loving, caring, compassionate, and merciful God. Let me suggest you pause and consider that it is not too late for you. I ask you to consider the message of the Bible of God's love, mercy, and hope. You can have hope if you place your hope in God. The message of the Bible is clear that, regardless of your past, God wants to forgive you. God will not give up on you!

This passage in Psalm 103 beautifully describes God's perspective on people that have failed him. At some point we have all failed God, but God tells us here that because of his mercy "he does not deal with us according to our sins", and even more than that he tells us that his love for us is so great that it is "as high as the heavens are above the earth" and he will not only forgive us of our sins but he will remove them "as far as the east is from the west!" What an amazing message of God's love, mercy, and forgiveness. I encourage you to embrace this wonderful message of the Bible that God wants to forgive you and that God will not give up on you. It is with this message that you can truly have hope.

Prayer for today:

Dear Lord, I thank you that you did not give up on me and that you have mercy on me even as one so unworthy. I humbly accept your forgiveness and thank you that I can have hope for another chance at life.

Notes of gratitude, progress, concerns, and prayers for today:

____

____

____

____

____

____

____

____

____

____

Day 10 of 100

You Can Change the Future

When Simon Peter saw this, he fell at Jesus' knees and said, "Go away from me, Lord; I am a sinful man!"...Then Jesus said to Simon, "Don't be afraid; from now on you will fish for people." [11] ***So they pulled their boats up on shore, left everything and followed him.***
(Luke 5:8,10-11 NIV)

After living a life in addiction for many years, there will probably be many things you've done that you hate to even think about, things that you wish you could forget. You may reflect on your past addiction and your actions to a spouse, or parent, or friend or co-worker and have regrets of all the people you hurt and the damage you caused to so many people. You will probably wish those memories would just go away and be forgotten forever because they are just too painful. That is all a part of your past and unfortunately, we cannot change the past. While it is absolutely true, we cannot change the past, it is also true that the past does not dictate our future. With God in our lives today, our future can be dramatically different from our past. As we seek his will in our life, we can change our future.

In this passage in the Gospel of Luke the apostle Peter came face to face with Jesus as the Son of God, Peter was then fully aware of his sinful condition and he fell on his knees and pleaded for Jesus to "Go away from me, Lord: I am a sinful man!" But Jesus had different plans for Peter. Jesus wanted a completely different life for Peter. Through faith in God, Peter was going to be an apostle and one of the founding fathers of the church; a very different life than he ever thought possible.

As you bring God into your life, you will likely also feel like Peter did when he said, "Go away from me, Lord; for I am a sinful man." But Jesus understands you and knows you are sinful and even so, he has different plans for you. Peter went from being a fisherman to a great leader of the church. Peter's future was dramatically different from his past. For you today, God has a future for you that is dramatically different from your past, one that you would never think possible before bringing God into your life. As you leave your past in the past and seek to follow God every day, you will see more and more of the amazing future that God has for you. You cannot change the past, but with God in your life, you can change the future.

Prayer for today:

Dear Lord, thank you for the forgiveness of my past sins and thank you that with you in my life my future can be dramatically different from my past.

Notes of gratitude, progress, concerns, and prayers for today:

____

____

____

____

____

____

____

____

____

____

Day 11 of 100

A Loving, Caring, and Compassionate God

The Lord is compassionate and gracious, slow to anger, abounding in love. (Psalm 103:8)

We all have different backgrounds, experiences, and views on God, religion, faith, and church. Our experiences growing up and our life experiences as adults may cause us to reject God, or to blame God for our condition, or to be angry at God for suffering the loss of a loved one. Many others view God as a harsh and mean-spirited God, always looking to punish us when we do something wrong. Others in recovery feel that God cannot forgive them; they believe what they have done in addiction is too "bad" for God to forgive them. Others choose to not believe that God even exists.

People in recovery and people in general will struggle with the idea of God. There are so many teachings and perspectives on God that it can be very confusing to know just how to view God. However, let me suggest these two simple and foundational beliefs about God I believe are taught throughout the Bible and are evident as we look at the world around us. One, there absolutely is a God. As we look at the created world around us, it is evidence that God exists. And second, not only does God exist, but he is a loving, caring and compassionate God; and he cares for you. These are two great truths! Not only does God exist, but he is a loving, caring and compassionate, God and he cares for you and for me. He is not a harsh, mean-spirited God, but a merciful and compassionate God. What great news for us to embrace and to be reminded of.

The passage from Psalm 103 today reminds us of these great truths, "The Lord is compassionate and gracious, slow to anger, abounding in love." First, this passage expresses there is a God by simply saying "The Lord" and second, that he is a compassionate and gracious, and loving God. If you have not considered God in this way,

I encourage you to reflect on these two great truths, that there is a God and he is a loving, caring, and compassionate God. As you progress in your recovery, one step at a time and one day at a time, always remember there is a God and he is a loving, caring, and compassionate God and he cares for you.

Prayer for today:

Dear Lord, thank you so much for being a loving, caring, and compassionate God and for caring for me. Help me to understand this more and more each day.

Notes of gratitude, progress, concerns, and prayers for today:

Day 12 of 100

A 'Pickle' Transformation

Therefore, if anyone is in Christ, he is a new creation. The old has passed away; behold, the new has come.
(2 Corinthians 5:17 ESV)

There is an old saying in recovery "Once you're a pickle, you can never go back to being a cucumber." It is a simple saying with a powerful message. For addicts and alcoholics, once you cross that line, you stop being a cucumber and you most assuredly become a pickle. You can never go back to being a cucumber again. Once you cross that line from a casual drinker or a recreational drug user to an alcoholic or drug addict, you can never go back. You will always be an alcoholic or an addict. This may sound like terrible news. But you can absolutely be successful in recovery, just as a pickle and not a cucumber. You can still live a life that is clean and sober and free of your previous bondage, but you will always need to be mindful you are in recovery. You are an alcoholic or addict in recovery. I encourage you to embrace this truth for yourself; it can be quite freeing and you may even be more open to helping others as well. Your life can be much more than just clean and sober; you can be in recovery and have a full and abundant life.

In a similar way, when you bring God into your life, you make a dramatic transformation; you become a child of God. Once you make this decision and bring God into your life, you will always be a child of God. You will see that you now want to do different things. Walt Heidecker, the founding pastor of our Discovery Recovery group, would say you get a new "want to". You now want to live a life that honors God. Gradually, your thoughts and actions will change as you genuinely want to honor God. You will still be an alcoholic or addict in recovery, but you will have a new "want to" one that seeks to honor God.

With God in your life, you can have a dramatically changed life. You can finally have success in recovery as a transformed man or woman of God with a new "want to". You can have peace in your mind, body, and spirit. Life will not be perfect, you will still have struggles and life will still show up. But continue on to trust God and to honor God and remember you are a "pickle", but you are a "pickle" in recovery.

Prayer for today:

Dear Lord, thank you for your transforming power in my life. Help me to always be mindful that I am in recovery as a "pickle" and thank you for giving me a new "want to" to honor you.

Notes of gratitude, progress, concerns, and prayers for today:

____

____

____

____

____

____

____

____

____

____

Day 13 of 100

Rest and Healing

Then, because so many people were coming and going that they did not even have a chance to eat, he said to them, "Come with me by yourselves to a quiet place and get some rest." [32] ***So they went away by themselves in a boat to a solitary place.***
(Mark 6:31-32 NIV)

After years and perhaps decades of addiction, there will be much damage to you physically, emotionally, and spiritually. Life in addiction will devastate your health and, in many respects, it will leave your entire being on life support. Even beyond your physical, emotional, and spiritual healing, there will also be healing needed in other areas for relationships, financial, medical, and many more. But early in your recovery, you need rest and healing. You need to spend some time in a safe, sober place with caring people who will help you get much needed rest and healing. The quote below from *Narcotics Anonymous* gives a vivid description of the devastation of addiction and how it will leave you tired, broken, and in much need of healing.

> "I was sick and tired and could not live with or without drugs. I wanted to stop using but did not know how. At that time I didn't know I had a disease; all I knew was that I could not stay a minute without using. When I couldn't sleep I would hurt myself so that physical pain would distract me from the distress I felt inside."[5]

You have been through so much, give yourself time to rest and heal. Yes, there are many areas that need restoration in your life, but right now the priority is to be in a safe, sober place and give yourself time to rest and heal. There are no quick solutions, your recovery will take time and that is absolutely ok. Do whatever is necessary to be successful in recovery.

In this passage in Mark, the scene described is hectic and full of much activity such that the disciples were being stretched physically and emotionally without even time to eat or rest. Jesus instructed them to "Come with me by yourselves to a quiet place and get some rest." This is the same message God has for you today, to go to a "quiet place and get some rest". Take whatever steps you can to ensure you are in a safe place and can get rest and healing and the care you need for your recovery. Leave the chaos of your past life in the past and bring God into your life so you can experience true rest and healing. Be open to God's leading in your life and he will direct you to just the right place where you can get rest and healing.

Prayer for today:

Dear Lord, direct me to a safe place for rest and healing. Help me to look to you for the ultimate healing in my life.

Notes of gratitude, progress, concerns, and prayers for today:

____

____

____

____

____

____

____

____

____

____

Day 14 of 100

There Are No Shortcuts

"What shall I do, Lord?" I asked. "Get up," the Lord said, "and go into Damascus. There you will be told all that you have been assigned to do." [11] ***My companions led me by the hand into Damascus, because the brilliance of the light had blinded me.***
(Acts 22:10-11 NIV)

Wherever you are in your recovery likely, you are thinking about the future steps and next phases of your recovery. You will perhaps make plans for what happens after you leave your recovery facility, or when you go back home, or get an apartment, or when you start back to work, or what will happen when you see family or friends again. It is human nature to want to plan and to make things go just a little bit faster. We often want to quickly jump ahead and perhaps even to take shortcuts. But do not skip any step of your recovery. At each phase along the way, embrace each part and do everything you are supposed to do. Take your medications, dialog with your counselors, read, pray, and learn as much as possible. Learn all you can at each step in your recovery. Do not rush your recovery. There are no shortcuts to your recovery, as your life depends on how much you learn in each part of your recovery journey. Each step of your recovery will help prepare you for the next step, so do everything possible to be as fully prepared for that next step.

This passage in Acts describes the beginning of the conversion event of the apostle Paul, where the Lord caused a bright light to blind the apostle Paul. The Lord used blindness to get the attention of the apostle Paul and then gave Paul instructions on what to do from that point forward to have his eyesight restored and to have his life transformed through a newfound faith in Christ.

Today, perhaps God used some event in your life to get your attention as to the fatal dangers of your addiction. Perhaps you had an overdose and had to be revived, or you spent time in prison, or you had a serious medical event because of your addiction. God wants to heal you and to have your life transformed through a newfound faith in Christ as well. But it is important you do "all that you have been assigned to do" for your recovery. Listen to your counselors, medical staff, and do all you can do at each step of your recovery. Don't take any shortcuts, but continue on one step at a time and one day at a time and be open to how God can use this time to heal you and even to transform you.

Prayer for today:

Dear Lord, help me to fully embrace each phase of my recovery and to do everything possible so that I will be completely prepared for my next step in recovery. Thank you for the caring staff and people you have put in my path to help me.

Notes of gratitude, progress, concerns, and prayers for today:

____

____

____

____

____

____

____

____

____

____

Why Doesn't God Just Heal Me?

I was given a thorn in my flesh, a messenger from Satan to torment me and keep me from becoming proud. [8] Three different times I begged the Lord to take it away. [9] Each time he said, "My grace is all you need. My power works best in weakness." So now I am glad to boast about my weaknesses, so that the power of Christ can work through me. (2 Corinthians 12:7-9 NLT)

It is a common question. Why doesn't God just heal me of my addiction? Why doesn't God just take away my desire for drugs and alcohol so I can easily be clean and sober? I know many pray for God to just take it all away, to take away any thought or craving for drugs and alcohol. Surely, God can see how this would be so good! Sometimes that is just what God does. Sometimes he works a miracle just like that and removes the desire for drugs and alcohol. However, it seems most often God does not work that immediate miracle of removing the addiction, but rather he works another miracle by giving the addict the grace to overcome the addiction.

In this passage, the apostle Paul describes "a thorn in my flesh". We don't know exactly what the thorn was. Perhaps it was a chronic illness, or a physical pain, or an emotional or spiritual challenge of some type. We don't know what it was. But, we know the apostle Paul prayed three times for God to remove this thorn, whatever it was. And it was so bad that Paul says "I begged the Lord to take it away." And yet God's answer was, "My grace is all you need. My power works best in weakness." How many times have you "begged" God to remove your addiction? God's answer may be the same for you today as for the apostle Paul "My grace is all you need. My power works best in weakness."

I encourage you today to accept God's miracle of grace. God's other miracle of grace to be successful in recovery and yet to still have the "thorn" of addiction. Then you can boast of your weaknesses and of God's power in your life; that you are a grateful addict, successful in recovery by the grace and power of God.

Prayer for today:

Dear Lord, I do ask you to heal me of my addiction and am willing to accept whatever your answer might be. I thank you for your promise of "My grace is all you need." I am grateful for your grace and power in my life.

Notes of gratitude, progress, concerns, and prayers for today:

____

____

____

____

____

____

____

____

____

____

Day 16 of 100

There Is a Solution

So I find this law at work: Although I want to do good, evil is right there with me. [22] For in my inner being I delight in God's law; [23] but I see another law at work in me, waging war against the law of my mind and making me a prisoner of the law of sin at work within me. [24] What a wretched man I am! Who will rescue me from this body that is subject to death? [25] Thanks be to God, who delivers me through Jesus Christ our Lord! (Romans 7:21-25 NIV)

Perhaps this passage describes how you feel right now. You want to do right, you want to be clean and sober, but evil is always right there close by. You love God and want to honor him with your life, but there is a war going on in your mind and body and you feel you are a prisoner of your addiction. You feel like a failed wretched person and you wonder if there is any hope for you. *Alcoholics Anonymous* speaks to this similarly when it states:

> "When this sort of thinking is fully established in an individual with alcoholic tendencies, he has probably placed himself beyond human aid, and unless locked up, may die or go permanently insane....So many want to stop but cannot. There is a solution....The central fact of our lives today is the absolute certainty that our Creator has entered into our hearts and lives in a way which is indeed miraculous. He has commenced to accomplish those things for us which we could never do by ourselves."[6]

You may feel that you desperately want to stop, but cannot. You may feel you do not know what to do or what the answer might be. However, *Alcoholics Anonymous* does not stop there as it continues and says that "There is a solution". *Alcoholics Anonymous* and this passage in Romans do not leave us as "wretched" people without hope. The apostle Paul correctly describes our wretched condition warring with sin, addiction, and many other failings, but Paul then asks the absolute right question 'who will rescue us?' The apostle Paul responds yes there is a solution, there is an answer, and there is hope. Paul declares, "Thanks be to God, who delivers me through Jesus Christ our Lord." There is a solution! You can be successful in recovery and it is by bringing God into your life and letting him direct your life in a way which is indeed miraculous.

Prayer for today:

Dear Lord, I thank you that there is a solution and it is through faith in the Lord Jesus. Help me to grow in my faith and in my recovery.

Notes of gratitude, progress, concerns, and prayers for today:

____

____

____

____

____

____

____

____

____

____

Day 17 of 100

God Does Not Condemn You

Jesus straightened up and asked her, "Woman, where are they? Has no one condemned you?" [11] "No one, sir," she said. "Then neither do I condemn you," Jesus declared. "Go now and leave your life of sin." (John 8:10-11 NIV)

Many individuals have said that through years of life in addiction, they have done so many terrible things they do not feel they can ever be forgiven. After many failed attempts at recovery, only to be followed by another relapse, many feel hopeless and broken. While they are full of remorse for their past deeds, they feel their family cannot forgive them, they cannot forgive themselves, and they feel God cannot forgive them. They feel hopeless and alone.

Perhaps this is how you feel today, hopeless, alone, and beyond forgiveness. This passage in John tells of the woman caught in adultery and everyone was quick to condemn her and her actions. In their efforts to trap Jesus, they were willing to leave this woman condemned and lost in her sin. They were willing to condemn her without hope and without forgiveness. Perhaps there may be some in your life that are quick to condemn you, but likely you are all too quick to condemn yourself first. But, in this passage after no one was left to condemn her, Jesus said to her, "Then neither do I condemn you." These are the same words Jesus says to you today, "neither do I condemn you." Please understand God will not only forgive you, but he is eager to forgive you! God simply wants you to ask him for help and to come into your life. With God in your life, there is always hope. There is always forgiveness and you are never alone.

Accept this forgiveness and bring God into your life. In this passage, Jesus ends by saying "Go now and leave your life of sin." With God in your life, you can have forgiveness of all your past sins with drugs and alcohol and any other sin. But, God also says for you to "leave your life of sin." It will not be easy, but with God in your life, it is absolutely possible. Cling to the message of this passage,

‘God does not condemn you’ and accept his forgiveness and then leave your life of sin and seek to honor God every day and you will have a brand new life in Christ.

Prayer for today:

Dear Lord, I am so grateful that you do not condemn me and that you forgive me. Help me to leave my life of sin and to follow you in a brand new life in Christ and in recovery.

Notes of gratitude, progress, concerns, and prayers for today:

____

____

____

____

____

____

____

____

____

____

Day 18 of 100

You Were Designed and Created by God

For you created my inmost being; you knit me together in my mother's womb. [14] ***I praise you because I am fearfully and wonderfully made; your works are wonderful, I know that full well.***
(Psalm 139:13-14 NIV)

One of the terrible teachings of modern popular culture is that we are all born by chance; random biological processes that somehow all came together to form us as an embryo and then eventually to be born. We were all just random creations with no design, purpose, or higher calling. It would then follow life itself would not have any meaning, purpose, or higher calling. Life would be empty and meaningless, only full of other chance random events and certainly then void of God as well. But what would life be like if this was true? Life would be empty, meaningless, and the God-sized hole we each have would remain empty. Yet, we would continue to seek various ways to fill this God-sized hole with drugs, alcohol, sex, money, and things of all types, only to always fall short.

This passage from Psalm 139 tells us we are all made by God! We are each created by God and we are each "fearfully and wonderfully made". What an amazing declaration! We are not created by chance random events, but we are designed and wonderfully created by God. God knew us as we were still developing in our mother's womb. God created you! You were not a surprise to God and even more than that, God has a plan and purpose for your life. Pause and consider that you were specifically designed and created by God. Consider also what were you designed and created for? What is your purpose in life? What is your higher calling? Does your purpose include being a godly man, woman, son, daughter, parent, spouse, or sibling?

Perhaps right now today you do not feel like a godly person. It is not too late. You can start today. I encourage you to start by seeking to bring God into your life. Ask God in a brief prayer to simply come into your life and direct your steps. God will begin to show you were "fearfully and wonderfully made" and he has a purpose and plan for your life. God will gradually show you the godly man or the godly woman he has designed you to be, and that will indeed be a wonderful thing.

Prayer for today:

Dear Lord, thank you that I am fearfully and wonderfully made and that you have created me for a purpose. Help me to see more and more clearly each day the plan and purpose you have for me.

Notes of gratitude, progress, concerns, and prayers for today:

____

____

____

____

____

____

____

____

____

____

Day 19 of 100

A Simple Prayer

Call to Me, and I will answer you, and show you great and mighty things, which you do not know. (Jeremiah 33:3 NKJV)

A dear friend in recovery shared his story one day, and he described when he was at his lowest point, when he was at his bottom. He felt hopeless, that he could not stop drinking, no matter how hard he tried. He felt he was doomed to live as an alcoholic and that it would not be long before it would surely kill him. He described his feelings of hopelessness and despair and that he did not know what else to do and so he called out to God, "God please help me!" It was a prayer of desperation. It was an honest prayer. It was a simple prayer. He finally accepted that without God, he could not stop drinking. He recognized he wanted desperately to stop but he could not and so he called out to God for help with a simple, honest prayer "God please help me!" God answered his prayer and several individuals came to his aid and helped him get to treatment. This dear friend is now successful in recovery for many years and is now giving back by helping many others and it started with a simple prayer.

The books of *Alcoholics Anonymous* and *Narcotics Anonymous* both have similar stories of this same type of simple prayer. *Narcotics Anonymous* describes one example as "One day, after nearly overdosing and reaching the point where I became 'sick and tired of being sick and tired,' I dropped to my knees and prayed that famous prayer, 'Please, God, help me.' I'm so grateful that God still hears an addict's prayer."[7] I want you to know that God still hears these desperate cries for help and God still answers these prayers today. But please be mindful God may answer your prayer in a way you do not expect or you do not think is best, but if your prayer is an honest prayer, you will be open and willing to yield to God's will in your life. As you pray this simple prayer, be ready to take whatever steps God may direct as you begin your journey of recovery, but this time as God directs.

The passage in Jeremiah is a great verse that corresponds to this simple prayer of "God, please help me!" This verse from God's Word instructs us to call out to God, and it makes the promise God will answer us. Even beyond that, God will respond by showing us great and mighty things we do not know. As you are open to God's direction in your life and in your recovery, he will show you things you do not know about yourself, but yet are critical for your recovery. I encourage you to be open and yielding to God's direction in your life as he answers your simple prayer of "God please help me!"

Prayer for today:

Dear Lord, I am so grateful that you still hear an addict's prayer and that you hear my prayer. Lord I am wide open to your will in my life. Guide me to the steps you want for me to be successful in recovery and to bring you into my life.

Notes of gratitude, progress, concerns, and prayers for today:

___

___

___

___

___

___

___

___

___

Day 20 of 100

Seek God and You Will Find Him

You will seek me and find me
when you seek me with all of your heart.
(Jeremiah 29:13 NIV)

Alcoholics Anonymous and *Narcotics Anonymous* have much to say about finding a "Higher Power" or "your own conception of God" or even God as we "understood him". For these fellowships, seeking and finding God is of critical importance to those seeking success in recovery. But neither fellowship will advocate any particular conception of God or any particular religious faith, just the importance of a Higher Power for recovery. Rather, you are encouraged to find your own conception of God and that this search is critical to being successful in recovery. Regarding this search for a Higher Power *Alcoholics Anonymous* states:

> "For faith in a Power greater than ourselves, and miraculous demonstrations of that power in human lives, are facts as old as man himself. We finally saw that faith in some kind of God was a part of our make-up....Sometimes we had to search fearlessly, but He was there. He was as much a fact as we were."[8]

This quote from *Alcoholics Anonymous* is like the passage from the prophet Jeremiah, who is also speaking about seeking God. Both stress the importance of searching for God with "all your heart." As you reflect on your current circumstance and your addiction, you may feel you are at the bottom and you are absolutely desperate for help. I encourage you to consider your quest for help should start with a sincere search for God and that you search for him "with all your heart". You do not need to concern yourself with all the doctrinal details of God, but simply focus on seeking God. The prophet Jeremiah was right many years ago, and it is still true today that "You will seek me and find me, when you seek me with all your heart."

How do you seek to find God? There are many ways to seek God. But, certainly they include: prayer (simple honest prayers), reading the Bible and other spiritual books, church (attend various churches and fellowships), faith-based meetings (Celebrate Recovery and others), and also seek wise counsel from godly trusted individuals. When you seek God with all of your heart, you will find him and your road to recovery can truly begin as never before.

Prayer for today:

Dear Lord, I pray today for your help. You know my circumstance and my great needs. Please reveal yourself to me as never before and help my faith to begin to grow in a newfound relationship with you.

Notes of gratitude, progress, concerns, and prayers for today:

____

____

____

____

____

____

____

____

____

____

Day 21 of 100

Jesus Is the True Higher Power

Jesus answered, "I am the way, and the truth, and the life. No one comes to the Father except through me." (John 14:5-6 NIV)

Many people, because of their life experience, have become disconnected from religion, faith, or anything associated with God. Unfortunately, even people that are considered great religious leaders may fail us, fail their faith community, and ultimately fail God. But, as we consider this truth of others, we need to also recognize that we ourselves fail people and also fail God. The world is made up of failed people, but that does not change the truth about God.

One of the great principles that came out of *Alcoholics Anonymous* is the idea of a "Higher Power"[9]. One of the founders of AA, Bill W., shares how this idea of a Higher Power started:

> "My friend suggested what then seemed a novel idea. He said, *'Why don't you choose your own conception of God?'* That statement hit me hard. It melted the icy intellectual mountain in whose shadow I had lived and shivered many years. I stood in the sunlight at last. *It was only a matter of being willing to believe in a Power greater than myself. Nothing more was required of me to make my beginning.*"[10]

Alcoholics Anonymous is very much a book about God in the life of people in recovery and makes clear the importance of having a spiritual experience. We don't need to fully understand who God is, but we need to accept that there is a God and he wants to help us in recovery. Any past bad experiences with religion can be replaced with simply accepting that there is a Higher Power and he wants to help us be successful in recovery.

In this passage, the apostle Thomas asks Jesus a probing question about the future. Jesus, however, answers the question with a great declaration about himself. In many ways, Jesus declares he is the “True Higher Power” by stating “I am the way, and the truth, and the life. No one comes to the Father except through me.” What a great declaration! As you seek to find your “Higher Power” I ask you to consider the words of Jesus “I am the way, and the truth, and the life.” Leave your past conceptions of God in the past and consider Jesus as “The True Higher Power”.

Prayer for today:

Dear Lord, help me to leave my past negative conceptions of God and faith in the past and help me to see you as The True Higher Power. Help me to start with a fresh new spiritual experience with the loving God of the Bible.

Notes of gratitude, progress, concerns, and prayers for today:

____

____

____

____

____

____

____

____

____

____

Day 22 of 100

Broken Relationships Restored

Be completely humble and gentle; be patient, bearing with one another in love. [3] Make every effort to keep the unity of the Spirit through the bond of peace.
(Ephesians 4:2-3 NIV)

Often included in the casualties of addiction are broken relationships. After years and decades of living a life in addiction there will be terrible damage to relationships with parents, a spouse, kids, extended family, friends, and co-workers. Once an individual starts in recovery, they will often talk about the many damaged relationships in their life. Some individuals in recovery will feel they have so totally devastated their family relationship that it is not possible to have them restored again. Others will feel they desperately want to restore their broken relationships with their loved ones and they want these relationships to be back to "normal" as quickly as possible. Perhaps you also want desperately to have your broken relationships restored.

God has made us wired for relationships. That is why the relationships with our loved ones are so important, why they matter so much, and why it hurts so much when they are not right. God is also all about relationships. That is why God so desires us to have a relationship with him. Regardless of what condition the relationships with your loved ones are in right now, seek God's direction for these relationships. But, first seek to restore your relationship with God. It is only once you have a restored relationship with God that you can really be prepared to restore relationships with your loved ones.

Also, be patient. Be patient with yourself and be patient with your loved ones. It will take time. As the passage in Ephesians says be "humble and gentle" and "be patient". I encourage you to be humble, gentle, and patient. It will take time for your body, mind, and spirit to get healthy and it will take time for your loved ones to begin to trust you again. Be patient and begin to nurture the relationships with your loved ones being mindful to be patient with them and yourself; and remember to treat "one another with love". Restore your relationship with God first, then you will be prepared to begin to restore the broken relationships with your loved ones as well. Just remember to be humble, gentle, and patient.

Prayer for today:

Dear Lord, forgive me for all the harm I caused my loved ones. Refresh and restore my relationship with you first and help me to keep you as my priority. Help me to be humble, gentle, and patient as you restore the other broken relationships in my life.

Notes of gratitude, progress, concerns, and prayers for today:

____

____

____

____

____

____

____

____

____

____

Day 23 of 100

People, Places, and Things

Blessed is the man who walks not in the counsel of the wicked, nor stands in the way of sinners, nor sits in the seat of scoffers; [2] but his delight is in the law of the Lord, and on his law he meditates day and night.
(Psalm 1:1-2 ESV)

Wherever you are at in recovery, it is important to be mindful of this common recovery principle of "People, Places, and Things". This phrase is a good reminder that it is important to always seek a place that is protected and safe for you to continue being successful in recovery. It may mean going back to your family or back to your own home, but it may also mean you need to go to a completely different area. If you are in a recovery facility, it is especially important for you to carefully plan where you go next when you complete your treatment. Work with your counselors, your sponsor, and other trusted individuals to determine where you should go after treatment. Be sure to consider what scenario will give you the best opportunity to be successful in recovery.

Surround yourself as much as possible with people, places, and things that reflect your desire to be clean and sober and that will strengthen your faith. Carefully, consider how to align these three aspects of your life in ways that are consistent with your desire to be successful in recovery and to grow in the Lord. For the "people" in your life, it is important to remove old friends and be intentional about making new godly friends. Likewise, it is wise to designate certain "places" as off-limits and add new "places" to your list to frequently attend, such as church, AA and NA meetings, faith-based groups, newfound hobbies or fitness activities and many more. In addition, consider the old "things" that should be removed and new "things" that should be added. Perhaps, consider the music, TV, movies, websites, and other social media that might need to be addressed. Carefully consider the people, places, and things that are consistent with your desire to do whatever is necessary to be successful in recovery.

These first few passages in Psalm 1 are really an Old Testament version of this common recovery principle of "People, Places, and Things". God made us and God understands us! His instructions for us were true 2000 years ago and they are still true today. I encourage you today to consider these two verses of Psalm 1 for yourself. Apply them to your situation and to your decisions regarding the "People, Places, and Things" that will give you the best opportunity to be successful in recovery.

Prayer for today:

Dear Lord, give me your wisdom to make the needed changes in my life regarding people, places, and things so that I can be successful in recovery and so that I can honor you as well.

Notes of gratitude, progress, concerns, and prayers for today:

____

____

____

____

____

____

____

____

____

Day 24 of 100

Bad News and Good News

For I am not ashamed of this Good News about Christ. It is the power of God at work, saving everyone who believes. (Romans 1:16 NLT)

There is a chapter in *The Big Book of AA* that tells the story of Dr. Bob and Bill W. as they meet with Bill D., the pioneer member of Akron's first group. They said to Bill D. "We've got some bad news for you. It was bad news for us, and it will probably be bad news for you. Whether you quit six days, months, or years, if you go out and take a drink or two, you'll end up in this hospital tied down, just like you have been in these past six months. You are an alcoholic."[11] That was devastating news to hear! But, the story did not stop there and does not need to stop there for you.

The story explains the principle of staying sober for twenty-four hours at a time. One day at a time was much more manageable and more practical. Another principle they shared with Bill D. was to bring God into his life and let God guide and direct his steps. These two principles were significant for Bill D. and his recovery. Bill D. eventually made a rather dramatic statement about AA and his recovery as he states:

> "I came into A. A. solely for the purpose of sobriety, but it has been through A. A. that I have found God. I feel that is about the most wonderful thing a person can do."[12]

At the time, the bad news was that he could never drink again, not even one. But, later through his sobriety, he discovered the truly good news. He found God and for him, that was the most wonderful thing possible. We can find 'the power of God' as we put our faith and trust in God. For you today, it may seem that living a life that is clean and sober is bad news, and you may feel it is not even possible. But, I encourage you to take it twenty-four hours at a time. As you continue on each day clean and sober and bring God into your life, you will see it is truly good news. You will come to see it is not only possible, but now with God in your life, it truly is the most wonderful thing a person can do.

Prayer for today:

Dear Lord, thank you for the Good News about Jesus and for the power of God at work in my life. Help me to focus on you and to trust you so I can be clean and sober 24 hours at a time and even one hour at a time.

Notes of gratitude, progress, concerns, and prayers for today:

____

____

____

____

____

____

____

____

____

____

Day 25 of 100

Not Even One

Therefore, get your minds ready for action by being fully sober, and set your hope completely on the grace that will be brought to you when Jesus Christ is revealed.[14] Like obedient children, do not comply with the evil urges you used to follow in your ignorance.
(1 Peter 1:13-14 NET)

There was a young man in our faith-based group who said he "needs to always remember that he is an addict, because if he ever thinks he is no longer an addict he will fall back into his addiction." That describes a harsh reality, but it was one he felt was important to his recovery. He recognized he will always be an addict, but an addict in recovery. Many individuals over the years have expressed how they started in recovery with the mindset to not drink or use at all and then, over time, they transitioned to thinking they could moderately drink or perhaps use softer drugs. Unfortunately, this thinking often led to a relapse and another stay at a rehab facility.

The recovery principle of "not even one" is critical to be successful in recovery. Artist Danny Simmons, founder of the Rush Philanthropic Arts Foundation, shared some of his experiences in addiction and his recovery in a Guidepost article. He described a time while he was in recovery, how he had terrible pain from hip surgeries and he wanted help and "thought I'd do heroin for one night, just to get some relief. One night turned into three years. Finally my family stepped in, but only after I lost my marriage and practically everything else."[13] To be successful in recovery, the principle of "not even one" is a change in thinking that is foundational. It is important to embrace this principle and hold to it firmly. Accept your limit as "not even one" and embrace it, as it will be your foundation of help in times of struggle.

It seems the apostle Peter might be giving a message directly to individuals in recovery as he talks about being "fully sober" and to "not comply with the evil urges you used to follow in your ignorance." Be fully sober and do not yield to the "evil urges" you had in the past and perhaps even have now. Do not yield. But, before your struggles come, "get your minds ready for action". Do everything you need to do to be successful in recovery. Get ready for action. Be ready, be obedient, be where you are supposed to be, and put your trust in God to help you when your struggles come. I encourage you to embrace the foundational principle of "not even one".

Prayer for today:

Dear Lord, help me to be fully prepared for when the struggles come. Help me to have the courage to hold fast to the foundational principle of not even one.

Notes of gratitude, progress, concerns, and prayers for today:

____

____

____

____

____

____

____

____

____

____

Day 26 of 100

You Are Not a Bad Person

But God showed his great love for us by sending Christ to die for us while we were still sinners. [9] And since we have been made right in God's sight by the blood of Christ, he will certainly save us from God's condemnation. (Romans 5:8-9 ESV)

There was a woman who had struggled with alcohol abuse for many years and she had relapsed yet again. She had tried to be successful in recovery many times, but she always relapsed. She was quite discouraged. When we met, I remember she was crying and she looked at me and through her tears said "I'm not a bad person." These words and her tears broke my heart. I assured her that, of course, she was not a bad person. But that is how she felt. She felt devastated. She had let her family down once again.

As we talked, I assured her that certainly she was not a bad person, not at all. But, even more importantly God did not think she was a bad person. In fact, God loved her and God wanted to free her of this terrible bondage to alcohol. She opened up to conversations about God as perhaps never before. She came to our faith-based recovery meeting that week and for the first time ever she declared, "I'm an alcoholic". She began to bring God into her life and she began the process of letting God direct her steps.

These two verses in Romans describe the simple message of the Bible. That God loves us and while we were still sinners, God sent Jesus into the world to save us and to make us right with God. In essence, they describe we are not bad people, but we are people in bondage to sin. God loves us and wants to save us from this bondage. For you today, you are not a bad person and God does not condemn you for your condition, for your struggle with drugs and alcohol. Rather, God loves you and wants to save you from the terrible condition of sin. I encourage you to bring God into your life. The simple message of the Bible is you are not a bad person, but you need freedom from sin. You are not a bad person and with God in your life you can be successful in recovery by grace through faith in the Lord Jesus Christ.

Prayer for today:

Dear Lord, I am so unworthy. Thank you so very much for loving me and for paying the price for my sins even while I was yet in my sin. Help me to understand that I am made right with God by grace through faith in the Lord Jesus Christ.

Notes of gratitude, progress, concerns, and prayers for today:

____

____

____

____

____

____

____

____

____

____

What About You?

"But what about you?" he asked. "Who do you say I am?" [16] Simon Peter answered, "You are the Messiah, the Son of the living God." [17] Jesus replied, "Blessed are you, Simon son of Jonah, for this was not revealed to you by flesh and blood, but by my Father in heaven."
(Matthew 16:15-17 NIV)

The Bible tells us that Jesus lived over 2000 years ago and many scholars throughout history would say no one impacted the world more than this one single person Jesus. However, many scholars of today, and the trend of the popular culture, deny the message of Jesus and some even deny he ever existed. Richard Dawkins, author of *The God Delusion,* attempts to make the case that God is a delusion and that God does not exist.[14] It may seem quite intellectual and advanced to make these claims, but perhaps it would be helpful if these modern thinkers could first answer a fundament question from the Bible that asks "Where were you when I laid the earth's foundation? Tell me, if you understand." (Job 38:4 NIV)

To deny God exists may seem freeing in some respects, but it actually leaves us quite lacking, empty, and with no guiding moral compass. If there is no God, then there is no right and wrong and anything goes and nothing matters. If nothing matters then nothing has meaning and we are left thinking life is meaningless. Perhaps, for a time, you lived your life as if there was no God? Or perhaps you simply rejected God and any thought of God. What was your life like during those times? While Dawkins did not arrive at the correct answers, I believe he attempted to answer the right questions. Namely, is there a God and who is Jesus?

In Matthew 16, Jesus asks the disciples this same basic question "Who do you say I am?" Peter answered for all the disciples saying "You are the Messiah, the Son of the living God." That is how Peter and the disciples answered this fundamental question of Jesus. This is a great question for us today as well. What about you? How do you answer this question? It is a question we all need to answer. Carefully consider this question for yourself as if Jesus was asking you directly "Who do you say I am?" How you answer this question about Jesus could be the key turning point in your life and it could lead to dramatically changing the direction of your life. Consider today "Who do you say I am?" With God in your life and Jesus as your Messiah and as your Higher Power, you can be successful in recovery and have a dramatically changed life.

Prayer for today:

Dear Lord, I thank you that you do indeed exist and that you are the creator of the world. Help me with my unbelief and help me to see in a fresh new way that you are the Messiah and the Son of the living God, the true Higher Power.

Notes of gratitude, progress, concerns, and prayers for today:

____

____

____

____

____

____

____

____

____

____

Day 28 of 100

Make a Decision to Put Your Faith in Jesus

For God so loved the world that he gave his one and only Son, that whoever believes in him shall not perish but have eternal life.
(John 3:16 NIV)

At times, individuals came to our faith-based recovery group who said they have not been in a church for years, some decades, and some have even said they were never in a church ever! There were many reasons given for why they had neglected church and God for so many years. Many expressed they never went to church as a child, some felt a pastor or other church leader left them down, some were angry at God for some past event in their lives, and some simply felt the church teachings were too focused on the so called 'rules and regulations' of that particular church. The focus was too often on what 'to do' and what 'not to do'.

Unfortunately, sometimes some churches and pastors lose focus of the primary message of the Bible. Over time, they focus too much on rules, regulations, programs, and policies and they tend to forget the world is full of lost and hurting people in need of the great message of hope that the Bible provides. They are not bad people or bad churches, but they have gradually moved away from the simple message of the Bible of God's great love for the world and his plan of redemption.

This passage of John 3:16 is one of the most well know verses in the Bible. The central message of the Bible is summarized quite beautifully in this one passage. It is not full of rules and regulations, but the simple message that begins with "For God so loved the world". It is because of this great love for us he provided a way of hope and redemption for us that would ultimately lead to eternal life for all who believe in Jesus. The simple message of the Bible is God loves us and he wants us to make a decision to believe in the Lord Jesus! This amazing message speaks of God's great love for the world, for us, and for you! Many today are still in bondage to alcohol, drugs, and other forms of sin and need this great message of hope. I encourage you to consider this passage personally for you "For God so loved you." The message of the Bible is not about a religion of rules and regulations, but about a relationship with God through faith in the Lord Jesus. Consider today for yourself this simple message of God's love and redemption for you. Respond to the great message of this passage, "For God so loved the world" and loves you and make a decision today to put your faith and trust in the Lord Jesus and bring God into your life and start a brand new relationship with God.

Prayer for today:

Dear Lord, thank you for your great love for the world and for your great love for me and thank you for providing a way of salvation and redemption. Today I put my faith and trust in you.

Notes of gratitude, progress, concerns, and prayers for today:

____

____

____

____

____

____

____

____

Day 29 of 100

Surround Yourself with Like-Minded People

Do not be misled: "Bad company corrupts good character." (1 Corinthians 15:33 NIV)

As you continue on in recovery, you will probably need to detach from many of your old friends. This is a good and necessary step. Embrace this step and be intentional and thoughtful with the individuals you need to detach from as "friends" from your phone, social media, and any other connections. Likewise, be thoughtful and intentional with the individuals you should add as "friends". These are action steps that are evidence of your commitment to do everything necessary to be successful in recovery.

This passage from the apostle Paul is just as true today as it was 2000 years ago. You have a choice to make, a decision that will absolutely affect your recovery. What type of people do you want to surround yourself? Do you want to surround yourself with individuals you know will eventually lead you away from God and back into your addiction? Or do you want to surround yourself with individuals that share your desire to be clean and sober and also share your love for God? The apostle Paul is absolutely correct if you surround yourself with bad company, it will corrupt your character and will gradually pull you back to addiction and away from God. But, if you surround yourself with good company, it will encourage your good character and will strengthen your recovery and draw you closer to God.

Intentionally consider your meetings schedule and plan your week with AA and NA meetings. Also, include faith-based meetings like Celebrate Recovery and others. Schedule your meetings for the week and then go faithfully to your meetings. Find a home church and then go to church every Sunday and yes, even go to Sunday School or perhaps a weekly Bible study! Surround yourself with like-minded people that share your desire to be clean and sober and share your love for God. You will develop new lasting friendships that will be with people that have good character and will help you grow in your recovery and in your faith.

Prayer for today:

Dear Lord, give me wisdom and the courage to establish the friendships you want for me. Help me to surround myself with people that share my desire to be clean and sober and share my love for you.

Notes of gratitude, progress, concerns, and prayers for today:

____

____

____

____

____

____

____

____

____

____

If Nothing Changes Then Nothing Changes

"But Lord," exclaimed Ananias, "I've heard many people talk about the terrible things this man has done to the believers in Jerusalem! (Acts 9:13 NLT)

The natural inclination of mankind is to gradually return to what we are familiar with, to do what we have always done. Usually this is fine, however, for the addict or alcoholic it is simply a recipe for relapse. Often the addict or alcoholic will need to hit bottom, or have some other event in their life that will cause them to seek help and often treatment in a facility. During these early days in recovery, they will usually make good and wise decisions to guide them in recovery. It is during these early days of recovery individuals will get needed medical care, valuable counseling, proper meals and rest, be surrounded by others also seeking recovery, attend meetings and church services, and certainly be in a safe and protected housing. But, as they go further into recovery, there is the tendency to gradually go back to what was done in the past. The old familiar people, places, and things will gradually return and with them also come the alcohol and drugs.

The challenge for individuals starting out in recovery is to establish new habits, new routines, and even new people, places, and things that support recovery. It is important to understand the recovery principle 'if nothing changes, then nothing changes'. Commit to make changes in your life and to do whatever is necessary for you to be successful in recovery.

In this passage in Acts, the apostle Paul is in the midst of his life-changing event of being blinded and being led to a man named Ananias to help him. Before this blinding event, Paul was a zealot seeking Christians so that he could arrest them or even put them to death. He was very much opposing Jesus and rejecting him, such that

Ananias was reluctant to help as he knew Paul and his past life. But, through this blinding event, Paul put his faith and trust in the Lord Jesus and made a decision to follow him. It was at this point in Paul's life he made dramatic changes. Paul left his past in the past and began to live a brand new life. This new life was very different from his past life. The apostle Paul went from a man determined to crush anyone professing Jesus to being one of the founders of the early Church and writing much of the New Testament. For Paul there was a dramatic change in his life after putting his faith in Jesus. I encourage you to bring God into your life and to consider what changes are needed for you to live a dramatically different life; a life that supports your recovery and also helps you grow in the Lord. With God in your life you can live a dramatically changed life.

Prayer for today:

Dear Lord, Help me to leave my past in the past and help me to make the changes needed so that I can be successful in recovery. Thank you for the promise that you will help me transform to a new person with a brand new life in Christ.

Notes of gratitude, progress, concerns, and prayers for today:

____

____

____

____

____

____

____

Day 31 of 100

God Made You for a Purpose

"For I know the plans I have for you," declares the Lord,
"plans to prosper you and not to harm you,
plans to give you hope and a future."
(Jeremiah 29:11 NIV)

Wherever you are at in your recovery, perhaps in a rehab facility, or a recovery house, or further along with several months clean and sober, I would like you to consider something a little different. Consider that God has made you for a purpose. You are gifted and wired with unique talents and skills only you have, and you are here for a purpose. You are not here just to get a good job and make lots of money and have lots of things. No, you are here on earth for a purpose.

There is a story of a young man in recovery who was living at home with his mom for a period of time early in his recovery, so he was in a safe protected place for a while. And he expressed to his mom he wanted to change directions in his life and she asked him a great question. She asked him "What has God called you to do?" That is a great question for each of us to consider. It is a great question for you to consider right now regardless of where you are at in your recovery. What has God called you to do? Consider the various skills, talents, and abilities God has given you and pray for God to lead you in just the right direction for your purpose. As you pursue this God-given purpose, you will experience a joy and satisfaction as never before.

What the prophet Jeremiah says here in this passage is still true today. God still declares to you, "For I know that plans I have for you... plans to prosper you and not to harm you, plans to give you hope and a future." God has plans for you and God has a purpose for you. God has called you for a special purpose. Consider today what has God called you to do? With God in your life and with God directing your life, you can have a brand new perspective and a brand new future. As you seek God's purpose for your life, you will see your life full of hope and an amazing future. Prayerfully consider that God made you for a purpose and then be open to his direction in your life.

Prayer for today:

Dear Lord, I ask for your guidance as to the plan and purpose that you have for me. Please begin to reveal to me your plan and purpose and guide me to begin the process to prepare for what you have called me to do.

Notes of gratitude, progress, concerns, and prayers for today:

____

____

____

____

____

____

____

____

____

____

Day 32 of 100

Life Will Not Be Perfect

I have told you these things, so that in me you may have peace. In this world you will have trouble. But take heart! I have overcome the world.
(John 16:33 NIV)

There are several major themes throughout *The Hope Recovery Devotional*. This devotional encourages you: to remember there is always hope with God, to do everything necessary to be successful in recovery, and to bring God into your life. These three core principles are major steps to being successful in recovery and to living a dramatically changed life.

However, while I absolutely encourage you to take these three steps and that your life will be dramatically changed it does not mean everything will be perfect. Sometimes we all have the subtle expectation once you are successful in recovery for a period of time and once you bring God into your life, then everything will be perfect. Now that you have done all these things for God, everything will be perfect. All of your problems will go away and God will dramatically intervene in a mighty way whenever you have a struggle, challenge, or difficulty. But one thing you can be certain of is there will be challenges in your life. Life will not be perfect, life will still show up! You can do everything right and sometimes bad things will still happen. There will still be bills, court hearings, medical issues, job issues, car repairs, relationship difficulties, long hours to work, and even tragedies of life.

The apostle John assures us that "In this world you will have trouble." Things will still go wrong. But, that is why Jesus told his disciples and even us today this passage of John 16:33, so that we would know to expect difficult times and we could still have peace despite having struggles of life. Jesus assures us with this same message today "But, take heart! I have overcome the world." You can be sure that in this world, you will still have trouble. Life will not be perfect, but with God in your life, you can have peace even in the midst of your struggles, because Jesus has overcome the world.

Prayer for today:

Dear Lord, I know that life will not be perfect and there will still be troubles, but I thank you that I can trust you to help me through the difficult times and struggles of life.

Notes of gratitude, progress, concerns, and prayers for today:

____

____

____

____

____

____

____

____

____

____

Day 33 of 100

Make a Schedule

Very early in the morning, while it was still dark, Jesus got up, left the house and went off to a solitary place, where he prayed. (Mark 1:35 NIV)

For many new in recovery, their journey will often include some time in a treatment or rehab facility. This is usually a very controlled and structured environment. The events of the day and week will all be planned out and schedules made for each individual depending on their specific needs. This structure, schedule, routine, chores, and oversight are important. But, often this structure, routine, and schedule is gradually forgotten when the individual leaves the facility and goes home or to some other living arrangement.

This passage in Mark indicates Jesus got up early to have a time of prayer. It suggests a quiet time of prayer was important and Jesus made time for it in his schedule. As you move forward in your recovery, it is important for you to find a safe and protected place to live and as much as possible to establish routines and schedules of things you determine are important for you to be successful in recovery. Certainly, I encourage you to consider making a schedule for a daily devotional time. Set a quiet time for you to be alone with the Lord in prayer, reflection, and reading of Scripture. In addition, I encourage you to set a daily schedule for the recovery meetings you will attend each day throughout the week. Include AA, NA, and faith-based meetings in your schedule. Write them down, put them in your phone calendar, set reminders, and then be determined to be faithful to that schedule. Your schedule of meetings should also include church on Sunday and perhaps even beyond that, possibly even to attend a Sunday School class or Bible study during the week.

Jesus got up early in the morning, left the house, and went to a quiet place to pray. What a great example for us to follow! Even today, consider what your schedule should be for this week and future weeks. When will you have your alone time with God or your daily devotions? When will you attend your daily or weekly meetings? If you have made the decision to do everything necessary to be successful in recovery I encourage you to set these events in your schedule. Consider your schedule today and then write it down, put it in your phone calendar and then do it beginning today!

Prayer for today:

Dear Lord, thank you for the example you set for us in your Word. Help me to set my own schedule for devotions and help me to be faithful to my schedule beginning even today.

Notes of gratitude, progress, concerns, and prayers for today:

____

____

____

____

____

____

____

____

____

____

Day 34 of 100

You Cannot Do It Alone

And let us consider how we may spur one another on toward love and good deeds, [25] not giving up meeting together, as some are in the habit of doing, but encouraging one another—and all the more as you see the Day approaching. (Hebrews 10:24-25 NIV)

God has made us as relational beings. We are at our best when we are living and functioning in a community in some manner, when we are in a group with a bond in some way. Isolation is the opposite of community. Isolation is generally not good for anyone, but it is especially dangerous for those in recovery. It is in isolation the addict or alcoholic will become depressed and vulnerable to relapse. In isolation they will have stopped doing all the things they had been doing to be successful in recovery and then that often leads to some very bad decisions. It is important to recognize that in recovery you cannot do it alone.

The AA and NA fellowships and faith-based recovery groups are great examples of community that provide a way for individuals in recovery to find encouragement and also to provide encouragement to others. These daily and weekly meetings provide the setting for people to get support from others facing the same battles. These fellowships are great ways to surround yourself with other individuals that share your desire to be clean and sober and also share your love for God. *Alcoholics Anonymous* talks about this bond in their AA fellowship as "There is no more aloneness, with that awful ache, so deep in the heart of every alcoholic that nothing, before, could ever reach it. That ache is gone and never need return again. Now there is a sense of belonging, of being wanted and needed and loved. In return for a bottle and a hangover, we have been given the Keys of the Kingdom."[15] You cannot do it alone, but you absolutely can do it in community supporting and encouraging each other.

This passage in Hebrews speaks about the importance of meeting together on a regular basis to "spur one another on toward love and good deeds” and by “encouraging one another”. Do not gradually fall into isolation, but stay connected to your meetings and groups. It is important to stay connected with others that share your desire to be clean and sober and share your love for God. If you have made the decision to do whatever is necessary to be successful in recovery, then also commit to a regular schedule of AA and NA meetings and faith-based recovery meetings. In addition, I encourage you to commit to a church you will consider your “home church” and then faithfully attend church each week. You cannot do it alone, but you absolutely can be successful in recovery as you stay connected with other like-minded individuals so you too can “spur one another on toward love and good deeds”.

Prayer for today:

Dear Lord, thank you for the blessing of community and of fellowship so that I do not need to go through life alone. Help me to support and encourage others in my fellowships.

Notes of gratitude, progress, concerns, and prayers for today:

____

____

____

____

____

____

____

____

Day 35 of 100

Be Strong and Courageous

Have I not commanded you? Be strong and courageous. Do not be afraid; do not be discouraged, for the Lord your God will be with you wherever you go. (Joshua 1:9 NIV)

The battle to be successful in recovery will probably be the most difficult battle you will ever face. Once a person crosses the line from recreational drug or alcohol use to addiction, it is terribly difficult to stop. When that line is crossed, you cannot go back. While you cannot go back, you can be successful in recovery, but it will not be easy. In fact, the battle of recovery is a life and death battle. Perhaps you have come near death yourself during your life of drugs and alcohol and perhaps you had to be revived with naloxone (NARCAN) or by some other means. To be successful in recovery, you will need to be strong and courageous.

The battle of recovery will be fierce, continual, and may include both setbacks and triumphs. It will not be easy, but victory is absolutely possible. The alternative is to give up, and that means certain death and devastation to all your loved ones. While there may be setbacks and perhaps even relapse, the only way you fail is if you stop trying. There is a story of a young man early in recovery who was committed to recovery. Every day at 7:00 in the morning, he would attend a recovery meeting. He did not drive, but every day he found a way there. Every morning at 7:00, he was at his recovery meeting. He eventually got a job and bought a cheap yard-sale bike so he could ride his bike to work. It was not glamorous, but it was what he needed to do to be successful in recovery. As you face your battle of recovery, I encourage you to honestly consider what you need to do to be successful in recovery.

In this passage today, Joshua is now the new leader of God's people after the death of Moses. The Lord is preparing Joshua for battle with the enemy of God's people. The words for Joshua are just as relevant to us today. It is important for us to remember what God has instructed us in his Word. It is important for us to be strong and courageous as we face any battle or challenge of life. It is important for us to not be afraid or discouraged; because we can trust God will be with us and will help us in any situation wherever we may go. I encourage you to bring God into your life so you can have the confidence to trust God, regardless of what you might be facing. As you put your faith and trust in God, he will enable you to be strong and courageous so you can be successful in your battle of recovery.

Prayer for today:

Dear Lord, thank you for your instruction to be strong and courageous and for your promise that you will be with me wherever I go. Be with me and help me today.

Notes of gratitude, progress, concerns, and prayers for today:

____

____

____

____

____

____

____

____

____

____

The Gift of Desperation

But soon a fierce storm came up. High waves were breaking into the boat, and it began to fill with water. [38] Jesus was sleeping at the back of the boat with his head on a cushion. The disciples woke him up, shouting, "Teacher, don't you care that we're going to drown?"
(Mark 4:37-38 NLT)

Unfortunately, it often takes dramatic and even tragic events in our life for us to understand we need to change. When these dramatic events happen, we realize we cannot continue on the way we have been going. We need to change or face certain death or other personal destruction. Perhaps you experienced some dramatic or tragic event in your life that has brought you to where you now know you need to take drastic steps to change your life. Often this dramatic event will be where you were near death by an overdose and you were revived by an EMT, or you recovered after many days in the hospital after a kidney failure, or losing your spouse, or losing your job, or finding yourself with overwhelming debt. It is dramatic events like these that often bring people to the point of desperation. Many in recovery refer to this realization as "the gift of desperation".

This passage in the Gospel of Mark describes the disciples and Jesus in a boat crossing the lake while a dangerous storm rose up, with strong winds and high waves, that were about to break the boat apart. The disciples were quickly facing a life and death situation. Jesus was right there with them the entire time, resting in the back of the boat. The disciples were desperate and facing death and so they called out to Jesus, "Teacher, don't you care that we're going to drown?" The disciples were desperate, but they knew who to call out to for help. They had tried all they could in their own power to fight the storm and to make it through on their own, but in their own power and skill and intellect, they could not steer the boat safely. And so, they cried out to Jesus for help. They were not sure what would happen or what Jesus would do, but they knew they couldn't make it on their own and they needed help and so they called out to Jesus for help.

Whatever your situation might be right now, I ask you to consider these same questions. Do you now understand you cannot do it on your own? Do you accept that in your own power and skill and intellect, you cannot beat your addiction by yourself? The disciples knew to call out to Jesus for help. Have you taken this same step and called out to Jesus? Jesus is right there with you and ready to help if you will simply call out to him. God cares that you are drowning in your addiction and God wants you to call out to him for help. I encourage you to bring God into your life, even though you may not be certain what a new relationship with God will look like. That first step can start with a simple prayer like "Dear God please help me." Do you want to do everything possible to be successful in recovery? I encourage you, even now in the midst of your storm of addiction, ask God to help you be successful in recovery.

Prayer for today:

Dear Lord, thank you for helping me in my time of need, when I am desperate for help. Please dear God help me in whatever way you feel is best and I will yield to your will.

Notes of gratitude, progress, concerns, and prayers for today:

____

____

____

____

____

____

Day 37 of 100

Be Patient with Yourself and Others

When Saul arrived in Jerusalem, he tried to meet with the believers, but they were all afraid of him. They did not believe he had truly become a believer!
(Acts 9:26 NLT)

Being successful in recovery does not happen fast. It takes time. You need to get help, you need to get physically healthy, you need to get mentally and emotionally healthy, and you need time. You will likely have a mix of emotions and thoughts and even doubts that you can even be successful in recovery. Perhaps you look back on your past life and all the damage you caused to yourself and others that you may feel it is impossible to be successful in recovery and impossible to restore the many broken relationships with your loved ones. To these very real concerns, you need to be patient with yourself and also patient with your loved ones. Recovery is a process, and it does not happen all at once. Your addiction did not happen all at once and your recovery will not instantly restore your life back to before your addiction. It will take time, but it is absolutely possible. Give yourself time and give your loved one's time too.

In this passage from Acts, the apostle Paul (as Saul) just had a dramatic encounter with Jesus on the road to Damascus when he was blinded for three days. At this point, Paul recovered his sight, and he expressed his newfound faith in Christ and became a believer. However, in the past life, the apostle Paul was quite violent towards the Christians as Paul was seeking them out to put them in prison or even put to death. Now, as a new Christian believer, there was a dramatic change in Paul's life and he sought to also proclaim the message of the gospel and not fight against it. But, the disciples were "all afraid of him" as they knew his terrible past. It took time for the disciples to see the change in his life and that it was a genuine change.

There may be some friends and family that are encouraged by your new steps in recovery, but they may be cautious to protect themselves so they do not get hurt again. Continue to do whatever is necessary to be successful in recovery and be patient with yourself, as it will not happen all at once. Also, be patient with your loved ones. It will take time for them to see there is a genuine change in your life and even then it may take even more time for them to feel it is safe to begin the process to restore their relationship with you. Be patient with yourself and be patient with your loved ones. But, be confident that with God in your life, even broken relationships can be restored.

Prayer for today:

Dear Lord, I thank you for your healing hand of protection in my life and I also ask you to help me be patient in the process of restoring the many broken relationships in my life.

Notes of gratitude, progress, concerns, and prayers for today:

____

____

____

____

____

____

____

____

____

____

Day 38 of 100

Just Show Up

Every day they continued to meet together in the temple courts. They broke bread in their homes and ate together with glad and sincere hearts, [47] ***praising God and enjoying the favor of all the people.***
(Acts 2:46-47 NIV)

Early in recovery, it is often easy to understand the need to get as much help as possible, including attending all the meetings, counseling sessions, and church services that are required and usually many more that are not required. To those that are serious about recovery, the need to attend all these sessions is painfully obvious, and the desire is there to attend as many as possible. But, as time goes on and you get further along in recovery, often there is a gradual change in mindset that you don't need to go to as many meetings as before. There is the thought you can pull back or perhaps even only go when you think you really need a meeting. While there will likely be a change in your schedule of meetings, counseling, and church services, it is absolutely critical this be an intentional and thoughtful decision. It is important to set your regular schedule of meetings, counseling sessions, faith-based meetings, and church services and then to be faithful and show up at each one on your schedule. Once you set your schedule of recovery events, then you need to simply show up. Be diligent and faithful and just show up. *Alcoholics Anonymous* describes this commitment for every day as:

> "So, here I am, sober. Successful. Serene. Just a few of the gifts of the program for surrendering, suiting up, and showing up for life every day.... I don't question how this program works. I trust in my God, stay involved in A.A. service, go to lots of meetings, work with others, and practice the principles of the Steps to the best of my willingness each day."[16]

In the passage today from Acts, the apostle Paul encourages the believers to continue to meet together regularly with "glad and sincere hearts" and "praising God and enjoying the favor of all the people." Gathering together with like-minded individuals is important as it nurtures the feeling of belonging, family, fellowship, and of a common bond together. It is important to show up at your meetings, faith-based meetings, and church services to not only be encouraged and supported, but so you can also encourage and support others. Be present so God can use others to help you and be present so God can use you to help others. Consider today ways to surround yourself with other like-minded individuals that share your desire to be clean and sober and also share your love for God. Make any adjustments to your daily and weekly schedules as you determine are appropriate and then just show up.

Prayer for today:

Dear Lord, thank you for the blessing of a recovery community. Help me to give back in service, encouragement, and support to those in my various fellowships.

Notes of gratitude, progress, concerns, and prayers for today:

____

____

____

____

____

____

____

Day 39 of 100

The Power of God

"Rabbi," his disciples asked him, "why was this man born blind? Was it because of his own sins or his parents' sins?" [3] "It was not because of his sins or his parents' sins," Jesus answered. "This happened so the power of God could be seen in him." (John 9:2-3 NLT)

Sometimes life does not seem fair. It seems some people have had very difficult and even tragic events in their life that just don't seem fair. There are times because of these tragic events some have turned to drugs or alcohol to escape, forget, or as a way to avoid having to deal with the impact of those events. Many individuals have shared the various difficult events in their life and how they then turned to drugs or alcohol. Some have lost loved ones, had devastating car accidents, chronic pain, difficult surgeries with long recovery periods, terribly dysfunctional home-life growing up, even losing a job of many years, and many more. But, what is often not considered is you can do everything right and bad things will still happen. Unfortunately, sometimes bad things happen.

What is important is how we respond to those events when they happen. One thing we can be sure of is bad things will happen. They have happened in the past and they will happen again. Sometimes we feel that once we are in recovery and even now have God in our life, we will no longer have terrible events in our life. But we can be sure that life will still show up, bad things will still happen even if we are in recovery and even if we are a Christian. But, as a Christian, we now know who we can turn to for strength, comfort, and wisdom when bad things happen. We know that we no longer need to turn to drugs or alcohol.

The passage from the Gospel of John describes a man who is blind, and the disciples asked Jesus 'why was he born blind?' Jesus responds that this happened "so the power of God could be seen in him." Jesus healed him of his blindness and restored his sight so the world could see the power of God in his life. For you and for me today sometimes bad things happen. But, whatever your past tragedy was, please know God can restore you from that past terrible event to reveal the power of God in your life. In addition, regardless of how devastating your past life in addiction was, God can heal you from your addiction and restore you to a brand new life in recovery. As you bring God into your life, he will help you be successful in recovery. God will use your past and your new life in recovery to display the power of God in your life so you can share that same wonderful hope with others that still need to know there is always hope with God.

Prayer for today:

Dear Lord, thank you for helping me when things go wrong. Please give me patience and wisdom to see how you are using my circumstances of life to reveal the power of God so that others may be helped.

Notes of gratitude, progress, concerns, and prayers for today:

____

____

____

____

____

____

____

____

____

Day 40 of 100

A Free Gift

For it is by grace you have been saved, through faith— and this is not from yourselves, it is the gift of God— [9] not by works, so that no one can boast.
(Ephesians 2:8-9 NIV)

As the result of the personal damage caused by years of alcohol and drugs, many individuals come back to reconsider matters of God and faith as part of their recovery process. The spiritual focus is sometimes done as part of the rehab facility, or as suggested by a counselor, or a family member, or as encouraged by the books of *Narcotics Anonymous* and *Alcoholics Anonymous*. The Twelve Steps of *Alcoholics Anonymous* and *Narcotics Anonymous* both speak much about God and is very much reflected in Step Three of recovery "We made a decision to turn our will and our lives over to the care of God as we understood Him."[17] Certainly, throughout this daily devotional book you are encouraged to bring God into your life. You are encouraged to believe in the Lord Jesus and you are encouraged to become a Christian. But what does it really mean to become a Christian?

Becoming a Christian is not about a religion of rules and regulations. It is not about abiding by a list of things to do and not to do. It is not about giving money every week and really it is not even about showing up at church every week. Becoming a Christian is simply making a personal decision to put your faith and trust in the Lord Jesus Christ. Becoming a Christian is putting your faith in Christ, becoming a follower of Christ, or becoming a disciple of Christ. This personal decision is an expression of faith and trust in the Lord Jesus. You acknowledge and have faith that what Jesus did on the cross was completely sufficient to pay the penalty for your sins. It is by this personal decision of faith you are then saved by grace. So becoming a Christian is an expression of faith in the Lord Jesus that you accept what he did for you on the cross of Calvary. This gift of redemption or salvation is a free gift! We do not need to pay any membership fees and we do not need to attend any number of days and there are no works of service that we need to complete. Salvation is a free gift of God. Becoming a Christian will change our hearts and will change our desire to want to honor God with our actions, but our actions do not save us they are simply the outward result of a grateful and humble child of God.

The passage today in Ephesians summarizes what it means to become a Christian "For it is by grace you have been saved, through faith...it is the gift of God." I encourage you today to consider making this expression of faith. Accept this free gift of God today by grace through faith in the Lord Jesus Christ.

Prayer for today:

Dear Lord, thank you for the simple gospel message that we can be saved by grace through faith in the Lord Jesus Christ. Help me when my faith is weak and help me to live a brand new life in Christ.

Notes of gratitude, progress, concerns, and prayers for today:

____

____

____

____

____

____

____

____

Day 41 of 100

One Day at a Time

In the day when I cried out, You answered me,
And made me bold with strength in my soul.
(Psalm 138:3 NKJV)

The phrase "one day at a time" is a common encouragement expressed to many people in all different types of difficult and challenging circumstances. But, it is perhaps best known as an encouragement and principle in recovery. Both *Narcotics Anonymous* and *Alcoholics Anonymous* use the phrase "one day at a time" in various ways. *Narcotics Anonymous* states "What a relief, when later I learned that it was easier by doing it just one day at a time....I would wake up in the morning and say, 'Just for today, I won't take anything,'"[18] This mindset is especially important for those in early recovery. Just focus on today, not the past, not tomorrow, not next month, and not next year. Just live another day, 24 hours, without using or drinking. Many have expressed a relief and even a feeling of accomplishment to lie down at night having another day, another 24 hours, clean and sober. Likewise *Alcoholics Anonymous* states:

> "The next question they asked was, 'You can quit twenty-four hours, can't you?' I said, 'Sure, yes, anybody can do that, for twenty-four hours.' They said, 'That's what we're talking about. Just twenty-four hours at a time.'"[19]

The focus is simply on one day at a time, not a whole year and certainly not the rest of your life, but rather just today, just 24 hours. The 'one day at a time' recovery principle is absolutely a great principle and has helped many throughout the years, but as powerful as it is it is even more powerful when combined with the power of God in your life. The verse for today in Psalms describes the psalmist king David with the confident declaration "In the day when I cried out, You answered me". What a great passage for us to embrace and to know every day we can call out to God for help and he will answer us! And even beyond that, he will not only answer us, but will make us "bold *with* strength" in our soul. God may answer our call for help in different ways. Perhaps he will bring someone to us, or we will get a phone call at just the right time, or some other means of help. But we can have confidence God will answer our cry for help. I encourage you today to consider a new routine for each morning to start each day off with an intentional focus on God. Start your new day "one day at a time" with perhaps a brief Bible passage, a daily devotional, and a brief prayer asking God at the beginning of this new day for help to live another day clean and sober. God has promised he will answer your prayer and make you bold with strength for your soul and for another day clean and sober!

Prayer for today:

Dear Lord, I thank you for the promise that you will answer me when I call out to you. Help me to take today as one day at a time and to look to you when I struggle.

Notes of gratitude, progress, concerns, and prayers for today:

____

____

____

____

____

____

____

____

____

Day 42 of 100

You Tried Everything Now Try God

When Jesus heard this, he said to him, "One thing you still lack. Sell all that you have and distribute to the poor, and you will have treasure in heaven; and come, follow me."* [23] *But when he heard these things, he became very sad, for he was extremely rich....* [26] *Those who heard it said, "Then who can be saved?"* [27] *But he said, "What is impossible with man is possible with God."
(Luke 18:22-24,26-27 ESV)

How many times have you tried to stop drinking or to stop using? How many times have you been in a rehab facility or in a recovery house? How many times have you said to yourself "that's it, never again!" Recovery is not easy. Once the line of being an addict or alcoholic is crossed, you cannot go back. *Alcoholics Anonymous* states it plainly it is not easy, but we are not left hopeless as it states:

> "So many want to stop but cannot. *There is a solution*....our Creator has entered into our hearts and lives in a way which is indeed miraculous. He has commenced to accomplish those things for us which we could never do by ourselves."[20]

So many want to stop, but it is just not that easy. It is perhaps one of the most difficult battles you will ever face in your life, but it is possible. Recovery is absolutely possible! That is the hope and truth you must never let go of. But, don't continue to try recovery by yourself. Don't continue to try recovery without God. Most likely you have tried many strategies to be successful in recovery and yet all have failed. Never stop trying, but now bring God into your life! Try recovery with God. You have tried everything else, now try recovery with God.

In the passage today from the Gospel of Luke Jesus is met by a rich man who asks Jesus how to gain eternal life. Jesus responded to sell all you have, give it to the poor, and then to 'come follow me.' The wealth and possessions of the rich man were his idols, and he was not willing to give up his idols. The rich man wanted to follow Jesus, but he wanted to still hold on to his idols. For you today, God does not want you to have any idols before him. The instructions of Jesus to the rich man are still valid for us today. For you to truly follow God, to truly bring God into your life, you need to turn away from any idols. You need to turn away from drugs and alcohol as idols and follow Jesus. Recovery is absolutely possible. There is a solution, but first you need to turn away from your idols. You cannot hold on to just social drinking or just softer drugs. You need to turn away completely and let God come into your life in a miraculous way to help you accomplish what you could never do on your own. "What is impossible with man is possible with God."

Prayer for today:

Dear Lord, I did try everything and now I ask you to come into my life and help me to be successful in recovery. I commit today to give up my idols and to follow only you.

Notes of gratitude, progress, concerns, and prayers for today:

____

____

____

____

____

____

Day 43 of 100

Be Where You Are Supposed to Be

If any of you lacks wisdom, you should ask God, who gives generously to all without finding fault, and it will be given to you. (James 1:5 NIV)

Some say that addicts are great liars. Unfortunately, addicts not only lie to others, but they also lie to themselves. Sometimes the lies are rather blatant and intentional, and sometimes the lies are more subtle and are closer to rationalizing than to lying. Occasionally I will be contacted by someone in our group who indicates they will not be at church on Sunday. Certainly, there are times we all need to miss Sunday church. But this should absolutely be the exception and not a common occurrence. It is important for us to be where we are supposed to be. When we calmly and prayerfully consider our schedule of meetings, church, and work, we need to be diligent and faithful and be where we are supposed to be. It is important to be where we are supposed to be! Unfortunately, addicts, and all of us, are inclined to rationalize our actions and behaviors to accommodate what we want. But all of us need to be obedient, faithful, and even courageous and be where we are supposed to be.

When we thoughtfully and prayerfully consider what God would have us do, it is usually plain how God would respond. If we pause and ask God the question we are considering, usually the answer from the Lord will be clear and direct. Often, we will know God's reply even before we finish asking the question. "Dear God, do you want me to go to my old friend's party where I know there will be alcohol and drugs or do you want me to skip it?" When we calmly express our prayer, we will often know the answer ourselves even before we finish the prayer. When we prayerfully ask for God's direction, he will provide it and it will usually be clear and obvious, but perhaps just not what we were hoping.

The passage today is a great truth from God's Word "If any of you lacks wisdom, you should ask God...and it will be given to you." The key is that we have to "ask God" because if we ask ourselves or others, we are not going to God for guidance. We are instead going to ourselves or to other people. I encourage you, for any decisions of your life, big or small, to "ask God" for direction. Ask God what he would want you to do and he will answer you. With God's direction in your life, you will always be where you are supposed to be.

Prayer for today:

Dear Lord, help me to be honest in my prayers and help me to clearly see your response to my prayers and then help me to have the courage to do the right thing and to be where I am supposed to be.

Notes of gratitude, progress, concerns, and prayers for today:

____

____

____

____

____

____

____

____

____

____

Day 44 of 100

'Stinking Thinking' Transformation

Instead, let the Spirit renew your thoughts and attitudes. [24] Put on your new nature, created to be like God —truly righteous and holy. (Ephesians 4:23-24 NLT)

A common expression in recovery is "stinking thinking", that over many years of life in addiction and living a damaging lifestyle, this "stinking thinking" had become a natural way of life. Your mind and heart had become conditioned to think and feel a certain way, in a way that has then been described as "stinking thinking". Many early in recovery look back and do not like the life they lived in the past and want desperately to be free of the addictive lifestyle, but they are not sure it is possible for them. Perhaps that is how you feel about yourself right now today. You do not like your past and you want desperately to change, but you are not sure it is possible for you. Let me assure you it is absolutely possible. *Alcoholics Anonymous* speaks to this topic when it states:

> "The great fact is just this, and nothing less: That we have had deep and effective spiritual experiences* which have revolutionized our whole attitude toward life, toward our fellows and toward God's universe."[21]

You can change, you can be successful in recovery, but first you need to be transformed by a spiritual experience. *Alcoholics Anonymous* describes this as a great fact and nothing less. It is important to understand a spiritual experience is not just some casual comment or going back to church or trying to be good. This great fact is a deep and effective spiritual experience where you turn your life and will over to the care of God. This is a spiritual experience where you put your faith and trust in God. This spiritual experience, then, will revolutionize your life in all your affairs. It will change your attitude toward your life, your friends and family, and it will change your attitude toward God.

The passage today from Ephesians speaks to this transformation. With God in your life, he will renew your thoughts and attitudes, he will renew your heart, and you will have a new nature. With this new nature you will want to honor God in your life, to do the right thing, and you will feel remorse when you fail God. These are signs God is working in your life, that he is renewing your heart, and that you have had a deep spiritual experience. I encourage you to continue to draw close to God and continue to let him renew your heart and mind so you move on from 'stinking thinking' to a brand new life with God.

Prayer for today:

Dear Lord, I thank you for your promise to rescue me from my old mode of "stinking thinking" and to renew my heart and mind to new thoughts and attitudes that honor you and lead me to be successful in recovery.

Notes of gratitude, progress, concerns, and prayers for today:

____

____

____

____

____

____

____

____

Day 45 of 100

We Admitted We Were Powerless

And I know that nothing good lives in me, that is, in my sinful nature. I want to do what is right, but I can't. (Romans 7:18 NLT)

Step #1 of Recovery

We admitted that we were powerless over our addiction, that our lives had become unmanageable.[22]

The Twelves Steps of Recovery, from *Alcoholics Anonymous* and *Narcotics Anonymous*, have helped millions of people to be successful in recovery. Millions of people are now successfully living a life in recovery with the principles of the Twelve Steps and they can also help you. Step One is really the most important step, because it is with this step all the others build upon. Step One will show if you are really serious about recovery. It is with Step One where you have the opportunity to start to be honest with yourself and to begin the journey of doing everything necessary to be successful in recovery.

Step One is all about admitting you are powerless over alcohol or drugs and that your life has become unmanageable. This is a dramatic and humbling admission, but it is one that you must honestly make to yourself and you must embrace this as your truth. Do not rationalize it away. It is not pleasant to admit this, but it is where you start with honestly admitting you are powerless over your addiction. Step One begins with the word "We" and this indicates that you will not go through recovery by yourself, you will go through it with others in the AA and NA fellowships, with your faith-based recovery groups, and also with your church. You still need to do the hard and at times painful work, but you will not be alone. In addition, God will be with you the whole way as well.

The passage in Romans describes the way you may feel about yourself right now. You may feel there is nothing good in you and that while you want to stop, you can't. This passage describes the condition of the addict, so many want to stop but cannot. You may feel hopeless. In reality, this condition is true for all of us before we brought God into our lives. We are all unrighteous; we all fall way short of God's standard. But, the first step to recovery and to a right relationship with God is to admit we are powerless over drugs or alcohol, and to admit we are powerless over sin. I encourage you to remember with God there is always hope. With Step One you have taken the most important step. Now continue in your recovery journey and do everything necessary to be successful for recovery.

Prayer for today:

Dear Lord, I admit that I am powerless over my addiction and that I have lived a life contrary to your will. Help me to continue the process of recovery guided by your direction starting even today.

Notes of gratitude, progress, concerns, and prayers for today:

____

____

____

____

____

____

____

____

____

____

Day 46 of 100

A Power Greater than Ourselves

For God is working in you, giving you the desire and the power to do what pleases him. (Philippians 2:13 NLT)

Step #2 of Recovery

We came to believe that a Power greater than ourselves could restore us to sanity.[23]

After you admit you are powerless within your own strength, your own ability, and your own power to stop drinking or using, you will likely be flooded with an avalanche of thoughts and questions all revolving around the idea of "ok now what?" At this point, I encourage you to continue to cling to the recovery principle of one day at a time. Don't rush things and don't jump ahead or take any shortcuts. In Step One, you admitted a great truth, perhaps for the first time, that your life had become unmanageable! Now give yourself time to begin the healing process for your mind, body, and soul.

The first step starts with accepting the truth about your addiction and now Step Two begins to bring faith into the picture. Allow yourself to believe there is hope, but not a hope in your own power or your own strength. Rather to believe it is possible, there is hope through a power greater than yourself. Allow yourself to believe there is a power greater than yourself that can help you to be restored to sanity. It is absolutely possible and there is absolutely hope, because there is a God in heaven and he is a loving, caring, and compassionate God. God does not give up on us and he does not give up on you.

Step Two is all about hope. You came to believe that a Power greater than yourself could restore you to sanity! That is hope, and it is the beginning of an expression of faith. Bringing God into your life takes faith and this Step Two is the beginning of faith. This passage in Philippians states that "God is working in you" what a great declaration! It is God's power and not our own power. Nurture this expression of faith in God. Call out to God with simple modest prayers such as “Dear God please help me!” or “Dear God please calm my mind and body and spirit” or “Dear God please forgive me for everything!” God will answer your prayer and you will begin to see there really is hope. You will see there is a power greater than yourself and you will see it is possible for you to be successful in recovery. I encourage you to embrace the idea of hope and the small expression of faith, a faith in a power great than yourself, a faith in God; faith in a God that can restore you to sanity.

Prayer for today:

Dear Lord, I am so thankful that you exist and that I can call on a power greater than myself. Please help me to seek you more and more each day.

Notes of gratitude, progress, concerns, and prayers for today:

____

____

____

____

____

____

____

____

____

____

Day 47 of 100

Made a Decision for God

For it is by grace you have been saved, through faith and this is not from yourselves, it is the gift of God. (Ephesians 2:8 NIV)

Step #3 of Recovery

We made a decision to turn our will and our lives over to the care of God as we understood him.[24]

In your addiction, there were probably very few people you could trust and probably few people that trusted you. But now, as you consider bringing God into your life, you view things differently. You know your life had become unmanageable, but now you also know there is a power greater than yourself and this power can restore you to sanity. That understanding brings much hope for sure. Step Three of recovery is all about making a decision. It doesn't mean you have it all figured out, it doesn't mean it will be easy, and it doesn't mean you now know all about God. But it does mean you have made a decision to trust God. You trust there is a God in heaven and that God does, in fact, exist. And even beyond that, you trust he is a loving, caring, compassionate, and merciful God and he cares for you. This is the God the Bible describes, and it is the God you can trust. The most popular verse of the Bible declares this principle stating "For God so loved the world...." (John 3:16 NIV)

Step Three of recovery describes making a decision to turn your will and life over to the care of God. What a great description of committing your will and life to God! However, for you to be able to make this type of decision, you must first put your trust in God. Even though you were not able to trust others in the past, I encourage you now to put your trust in God, because you can trust God. This step requires faith. Faith that you can trust God and that he will come into your life, forgive you of your past, and that he will restore you. This decision is another way of making an expression of faith that you can trust God. Consider Step Three again as making an expression of faith.

Faith in God is what the message of the Bible is all about. You do not need to understand the whole Bible or have all the answers to all the questions of God and the Bible, but what you do need is an expression of faith in the Lord Jesus Christ. This expression of faith is made by grace, as our passage for today states "For it is by grace you have been saved, through faith...." I encourage you to make this decision to trust God by grace through faith in the Lord Jesus Christ. Make this decision today to turn your will and your life over to the care of God and then trust God one day at a time.

Prayer for today:

Dear Lord, today I humbly and gratefully make this expression of faith and put my faith and trust in the Lord Jesus. I ask you to come into my life and guide and direct me as I turn my will and my life over to you.

Notes of gratitude, progress, concerns, and prayers for today:

____

____

____

____

____

____

____

____

____

Day 48 of 100

Made a Fearless Moral Inventory

Search me, God, and know my heart; test me and know my anxious thoughts. 24 See if there is any offensive way in me, and lead me in the way everlasting.
(Psalm 139:23-24 NIV)

Step #4 of Recovery
We made a searching and fearless moral inventory of ourselves.[25]

The first three steps of *Alcoholics Anonymous* and *Narcotics Anonymous* are focused on your relationship with God. Step four begins looking inward honestly to see and understand your moral inventory. As in an inventory at a business or store, it is important to assess what is there. What is present both bad and good? With God in your life, he will help you make this searching and fearless inventory not only of your good and bad characteristics, but also of some of the significant events in your life that helped shape who you are today. Some of these events you were responsible for and some happened to you, but they all work together to make you who you are today.

A "searching" process means it will take effort. It will not be easy and will often require you to consider things that are not readily obvious. They are buried and you will need to attempt to honestly search for them. "Fearless" indicates it will take commitment to make this inventory of things, events, and actions in your life that will not be pleasant. Things that you wish you could forget ever happened. But God will give you the courage to make this inventory list that will ultimately strengthen your recovery. Please understand, regardless of the negative aspects of your past and of your moral inventory, that does not change the fact God loves you. God is a loving, caring, compassionate, and merciful God and he wants you to turn these terrible and often painful events of your past over to him and he will forgive you. We are all sinners and we all fall short of the glory of God and we are all eternally grateful that he forgives us from of our past no matter how terrible and painful.

The passage from Psalm 139 is a prayer asking God to help with this searching process, a process that was appropriate long ago and even today. "Search me, God, and know my heart...." God will help you with this searching process and he will help reveal the inner parts of your heart that might show the offensive ways of your past towards others, towards yourself, and even towards God. God will use this moral inventory for healing and forgiveness and a deeper relationship with the God of heaven. Make your searching and fearless moral inventory knowing God wants to help you as you leave your past in the past and look forward to a brand new life in Christ, a life very different from your past.

Prayer for today:

Dear Lord, give me the courage to search my heart to do an honest and fearless moral inventory and then help me to understand that you still love me despite my moral inventory.

Notes of gratitude, progress, concerns, and prayers for today:

____

____

____

____

____

____

____

____

____

Day 49 of 100

We Admitted to God Our Wrongs

Then I acknowledged my sin to you and did not cover up my iniquity. I said, "I will confess my transgressions to the Lord." And you forgave the guilt of my sin.
(Psalm 32:5 NIV)

<u>Step #5 of Recovery</u>
We admitted to God, to ourselves, and to another human being, the exact nature of our wrongs.[26]

The Twelve Steps of Recovery are not easy, but they have demonstrated to be tremendously helpful for millions of people over many decades of time. One of the main reasons the Twelve Steps have been so helpful is because they bring God into the picture. We are physical beings for sure, but we are also spiritual beings and our spiritual component needs to be addressed just as much as our physical body. Step Five is a difficult step. Most people do not like to admit being wrong, to God, to ourselves, or to anyone else. But that is what Step Five requires. After the moral inventory of Step Four, now Step Five instructs us to admit to God, ourselves, and another human being our wrongs!

Admit our wrongs sounds pretty harsh, perhaps even old fashioned or maybe too traditional to be appropriate for modern day people. Surely, there must be another way! But confession is good for the soul. Confession is good for our spiritual healing, just as sobriety, medicine, rest, and counseling are good for our physical body. Confessing to God is where our spiritual healing starts, and then it continues with confessing to ourselves. Confessing to ourselves is admitting and accepting responsibility for what we have done in the past, our wrongdoings, and our sin. Confessing to another trusted human being is beneficial in several ways. Verbalizing our sins and getting them out can be a helpful and even therapeutic for our soul.

Also, confessing our sins to God and to another human being is biblical. Psalm 32:5 describes this basic process of acknowledging our sin and confessing it to God, and then the most amazing part is

God will forgive us of our sins! God will forgive us of our wrongs. Step Five is all about confessing our wrongs to God, to ourselves, and to another human being so we can be forgiven. We do not have to hold on to the baggage of our past, of our past sins, rather, we can be forgiven. God is a loving, caring, compassionate, and merciful God and he is eager for us to turn back to him and for us to confess our sins. God very much wants to forgive us if we will only confess our sins to him. Don't wait any longer. Confess your sins to God, to yourself, and to a trusted individual and accept God's forgiveness.

Prayer for today:

Dear Lord, help me to be faithful and to bring all my sins before you in an honest way and not skipping over significant areas of sin. Guide me to just the right trusted individual for me to share the exact nature of my wrongs.

Notes of gratitude, progress, concerns, and prayers for today:

____

____

____

____

____

____

____

____

____

Day 50 of 100

Ready for God to Remove Our Defects

I will give them a new heart and a new mind.
I will take away their stubborn heart of stone
and will give them an obedient heart.
(Ezekiel 11:19 GNT)

Step #6 of Recovery
We were entirely ready to have God remove all these defects of character.[27]

Step Six is all about being ready for change. But, it is not change we make ourselves. If we had the power to make the changes ourselves, we would have done it long ago, but we do not have that kind of power. But God does have that power. Our part is to be ready and willing for God to remove all our character defects; not all at once but one at a time. It is not a race, but rather a journey; a journey with God now at the controls of our life. It may be difficult to give up some of the defects as we may have held on to them thinking we needed them, but now we recognize they are part of our problem.

The book *A Spiritual Kindergarten: Christian Perspectives on the Twelve Steps* says "Change is difficult. Even changes that we want to make are difficult. So we need to prepare ourselves for the change process.... It is time to prepare for God to do spiritual and psychological surgery on our character."[28] Spiritual and psychological surgery is a great description of the work God will be doing in our lives. God, as the great physician is doing the surgery on you as the patient who is ready and willing for surgery, but it is God doing the work.

The passage from Ezekiel corresponds to this idea of spiritual surgery. Ezekiel says that God will give them "a new heart and a new mind." That is just what we are asking of God in Step Six to remove our defects, to give us a new mind and ultimately to change our heart. As we grow in the Lord and we allow God to change us, we will more and more change from a "stubborn heart" and the Lord will give us an "obedient heart." It will not be easy and it will not be quick, but with God in our life, and if we are ready and willing, God will remove all our defects of character. One at a time and day by day, God will remove our defects as we continue to grow in the Lord and continue to be ready and willing. I encourage you to be patient with yourself and remember it is not a race, it is a journey. As you continue on with God in your life, he will give you a new heart and he will remove your defects of character and you will begin to see the change in your life with a new "obedient heart" that seeks to honor God.

Prayer for today:

Dear Lord, I bring myself before you to do your spiritual surgery to transform my heart and mind. Help me to be open to your work in my life to give me a new heart and a new mind.

Notes of gratitude, progress, concerns, and prayers for today:

____

____

____

____

____

____

____

____

____

____

Day 51 of 100

Humbly Ask God

If we confess our sins, he is faithful and just to forgive us our sins and to cleanse us from all unrighteousness. (1 John 1:9 ESV)

Step #7 of Recovery
We humbly asked Him to remove our shortcomings.[29]

It is not always easy to ask for help and in some ways, it is humbling. We acknowledge we cannot remove our shortcomings on our own and we need help from someone else. But Step Seven says we do it "humbly"! Not in humiliation or in failure, but understanding that asking God is absolutely the right thing to do. The one we are asking is the one who is fully ready, willing, and able to remove our shortcomings. We ask humbly, not in defeat, but with joyful expectation that God will remove our shortcomings in his timeframe.

Step Seven is a simple prayer with all the right components. We humbly ask God to remove our shortcomings. We humble ourselves to do the next right thing, which in this case is to ask for help. We wisely ask God to remove our shortcomings. The word "shortcomings" is another way of saying sin. The prayer does not ask God to help us manage our shortcomings or to better accommodate our shortcomings; but this simple prayer asks God to "remove" our shortcomings!

The passage for today describes the confidence we can have in God when we confess our sins to him, or when we confess our shortcomings to him. The passage says "he is faithful and just to forgive us our sins". Wow, that is a very confident declaration of God's faithfulness! Not only that, but God will "cleanse us" from everything we've done wrong. It may not be easy for you to accept this forgiveness or you may feel you do not deserve the forgiveness. And you would be correct, you do not deserve the forgiveness and neither do I or anyone else, but this promise is true and is a consistent message of the Bible. Now humbly accept God's forgiveness and embrace this as a truth from God's Word. Humbly ask God to remove your shortcomings and humbly accept his forgiveness and then humbly express your gratitude to God. Be grateful to God for removing your shortcomings and then continue on to live a brand new life, very different from your past.

Prayer for today:

Dear Lord, I humbly ask you to remove my many shortcomings and thank you for cleansing me of all my past sins. Help me to accept this great promise and to seek to honor you from this day forward.

Notes of gratitude, progress, concerns, and prayers for today:

____

____

____

____

____

____

____

____

____

____

Became Willing to Make Amends

What a wretched man I am! Who will rescue me from this body that is subject to death? [25] Thanks be to God, who delivers me through Jesus Christ our Lord! (Romans 7:24-25 NIV)

Step #8 of Recovery
We made a list of all persons we had harmed, and became willing to make amends to them all.[30]

The Twelve Steps of Recovery are all about restoration. The four main sections of the Twelve Steps each focus on a particular area of restoration: Steps One through Three are about restoring our relationship with God, Steps Four through Seven are about restoring peace within ourselves, and Steps Eight through Ten are about restoring relationships with others, and Steps Eleven and Twelve are about continuing this restoration and peace in the future.

Step Eight can be difficult and challenging. But it is important to remember Step Eight is not about who hurt us, it is not about us telling others how they offended us, and it is not about us trying to make other people like us again. Step Eight is focused on simply making a list of people we have harmed. We do not need to actually make the amends, but we need to make the list. This list can be quite helpful and yet troubling, as we list all the people we have harmed. But it might make us more willing to forgive others as we see the list of all the ones we have harmed.

As we make this list of the people we have harmed and remember the details of what happened during that event and all the many other events, we may conclude that we are a very bad person, even a terrible person. We may conclude just what our passage for today stated "What a wretched man I am!" And this statement is true for you, and for me, and for all of us! However, this passage does not leave us without hope but it provides us with the solution that "Thanks be to God, who delivers me through Jesus Christ our Lord!" What a great message of hope, forgiveness, and restoration. God does not leave us lost in our sin with no remedy and without hope, but God has provided the solution. Even when we were lost in our sin, and in our broken condition, God provided the way of restoration and forgiveness for you, and for me, and for all of us through the Lord Jesus Christ. God simply wants you to accept the free gift of salvation and of forgiveness for the sins of your past life as "a wretched" person and put your faith and trust in the Lord Jesus Christ by grace through faith. Step Eight will not be easy, but continue on with the list of Step Eight and pray for God's wisdom, guidance, and for relationships to be restored.

Prayer for today:

Dear Lord, give me your wisdom as I create this list of persons I have harmed and give me a heart of compassion to prepare me to make amends.

Notes of gratitude, progress, concerns, and prayers for today:

____

____

____

____

____

____

____

____

____

Day 53 of 100

Made Amends Wherever Possible

But Zacchaeus stood up and said to the Lord, "Look, Lord! Here and now I give half of my possessions to the poor, and if I have cheated anybody out of anything, I will pay back four times the amount." [9] Jesus said to him, "Today salvation has come to this house." (Luke 19:8-9 NIV)

<u>Step #9 of Recovery</u>

We made direct amends to such people wherever possible, except when to do so would injure them or others.[31]

Step Nine will be difficult. It is difficult because it involves meeting in person with someone we have harmed and actually making amends to this individual. While Step Nine is difficult, it can also be one of the most rewarding steps as well. It is important for us to have the proper mindset as we meet with this individual. We are there to express our remorse for how we harmed them and to make amends in a manner that is appropriate for the harm we caused. We need to be humble and sensitive to the other person and only make the amends if it will not injure them or others. *Narcotics Anonymous* gives this guidance "We approach those we have harmed with humility and patience.... We must remember the pain that they have known. In time, many miracles will occur."[32]

This is an important step for us to take. We need to understand we cannot control how the other person will respond, but we can control how we prepare, what we say, and how we present our remorse and amends. *Narcotics Anonymous* indicates it may be painful for us and likely for the other person, but it may also be miraculous! We need to be patient with ourselves and others and only take this step when we are ready and appropriate for us and the other person. The book *A Spiritual Kindergarten: Christian Perspectives on the Twelve Steps* expresses nicely the spiritual growth that is reflected in this step, stating "Step Nine invites us to develop empathy—the capacity to anticipate how others will be affected by our amends. This is exactly the quality of character that we lacked at the time that we did the harm we are now seeking to undo."[33]

The passage today from Luke 19 is about Zacchaeus, a man who came to Jesus whole heartedly, and was willing to do whatever was necessary for him to make amends to the people he had harmed. There is joy and an eagerness as Zacchaeus exclaims he was willing "Here and now" to make his amends. Are you ready to do whatever is necessary to make your amends? Are you ready to do whatever is necessary for you to be successful in recovery? Are you ready to do whatever is necessary to be an obedient and joyful follower of Jesus? Have a humble spirit and then go make your amends.

Prayer for today:

Dear Lord give me your wisdom and insight as I prepare to make amends to people I have harmed in the past. Give me just the right words and humble spirit as I make my amends.

Notes of gratitude, progress, concerns, and prayers for today:

____

____

____

____

____

____

____

____

____

Continue to Take Personal Inventory

If we say that we have no sin, we deceive ourselves, and the truth is not in us. [9] If we confess our sins, He is faithful and just to forgive us our sins and to cleanse us from all unrighteousness.
(1 John 1:8-9 NKJV)

Step #10 of Recovery
We continued to take personal inventory and when we were wrong promptly admitted it.[34]

Step Ten now moves us to a new focus of the Twelve Steps of Recovery to more of a focus on daily living. There are four main points of Step Ten. First, the word "continued" of Step Ten indicates an ongoing process, a daily process. It sets the model of an action that we take daily, to take personal inventory. In recovery and in our Christian walk, the process is very much one day at a time. The second key focus is to "take a personal inventory" of our thoughts, words, and actions where we sinned and failed God during the day. Then the third key is to recognize the times when we were wrong. This can be a humbling experience, but that is a good character trait and indicates growth from our past. With these wrongs identified, we then take the fourth key action of Step Ten and promptly admit our wrongs. Bring our sins and personal failures to God and ask him for forgiveness and guidance so we do not fall into those same sins again.

The passage for today from the first epistle of John brings out Step Ten similarly. This passage implies a time of humble and honest self-reflection where we recognize our sin and simply confess it to God. The apostle John likely intends for this to be a regular daily process. But, this passage takes our reflection and confession even further than is stated in Step Ten. This passage describes the great assurance we can have when we confess our sins. God "is faithful and just to forgive us our sins and to cleanse us from all unrighteousness."

God does not hang on to our wrongs. God does not record our sins to remind us later. God does not keep an ever growing list of our wrongs, but he cleanses our sins and our wrongs completely! We need to understand that God does not hang on to our wrongs. God does not hang on to our past and neither should we. This is a hard point, but we need to trust the Bible and what the Word of God states, "If we confess our sins, He is faithful and just to forgive us our sins and to cleanse us from all unrighteousness." What a great truth of God's Word. I encourage you to embrace this great truth and integrate this step into your life on a daily basis. This will enable you to continue to grow in your recovery and to also grow in your walk with the Lord.

Prayer for today:

Dear Lord, help me to have a humble and honest spirit as I reflect each day on my personal inventory. Help me to simply admit them and ask you for forgiveness and not to rationalize them away.

Notes of gratitude, progress, concerns, and prayers for today:

____

____

____

____

____

____

____

____

Day 55 of 100

Through Prayer and Meditation

Pray then like this: "Our Father in heaven, hallowed be your name. [10] Your kingdom come, your will be done, on earth as it is in heaven."
Matthew (6:9-10 ESV)

Step #11 of Recovery

We sought through prayer and meditation to improve our conscious contact with God as we understood Him, praying only for knowledge of His will for us and the power to carry that out.[35]

Step Eleven is one of the "maintenance" steps, and it all centers on prayer and meditation. Just as with Step Ten, it is implied that it is a regular event, a daily process. The principles of this step are really quite foundational to our recovery and to our walk with the Lord. Daily we are to pray to God and then to meditate and take time to listen for God's response to our prayer. But, the prayers are not just random or self-centered prayers rather, they are quite specific prayers for three things: to improve our conscious contact with God, for knowledge of his will, and for the power to carry that out. These prayers are likely very different from any prayers we might have prayed in the past in our addiction. This new prayer of Step Eleven takes the focus off of us and on to God and his will in our life. Actually, it can be quite freeing to 'let go and let God' be the one in charge of our life.

The passage for today from Matthew is the beginning of the Lord's Prayer. Jesus gives the disciples an example of how to pray. It indicates a tender relationship with a loving father starting with "Our Father". The focus is on God and his will. This is the model Jesus gave his disciples and now even to us so we know how to pray. It is important to remember God is our loving father. He is a loving, caring, and compassionate God who wants to help us, to forgive us, and to have a restored relationship with us. The Lord's prayer also indicates we are to honor God with our life and we can do this best by knowing his will and then by actually living his will out in our life.

This is not easy, but with God's strength we can live a dramatically different life. I encourage you to find a time every day to pray and to take time to meditate and listen for God's response. As you improve your conscious contact with God you will know his will for your life more and more clearly and then with God's power you can live it out one day at a time.

Prayer for today:

Dear Lord, I thank you that I can come to you in prayer as my heavenly father. Help me to know your will for me each day and give me to the power to carry out your will in my life.

Notes of gratitude, progress, concerns, and prayers for today:

____

____

____

____

____

____

____

____

____

____

Day 56 of 100

Had a Spiritual Awakening

Jesus answered and said to him, "Most assuredly, I say to you, unless one is born again, he cannot see the kingdom of God."
(John 3:3 NKJV)

Step #12 of Recovery
Having had a spiritual awakening as a result of these steps, we tried to carry this message to addicts, and to practice these principles in all our affairs.[36]

Step Twelve is the last of the Twelve Steps, but it certainly is not the end of the steps. The Twelves Steps are principles of life. They are principles of life for individuals in recovery and can be embraced by all Christians as well. The Twelve Steps are built on biblical principles and are all about a spiritual change or a spiritual awakening if you will. Without a spiritual awakening, Step Twelve is meaningless. Many were spiritually dead, spiritually empty, or spiritually asleep. But, through the Twelve Steps and through a spiritual rebirth by grace through faith in Christ, many have now had a spiritual awakening and are being transformed by a new life in Christ. Through the Twelve Steps and through a spiritual awakening, many can now be successful in recovery. It is still a day by day process, but we now know with God in our life it is possible to be successful in recovery. We now know God will do for us what we were powerless to do for ourselves.

It is with this spiritual awakening we now have a message of hope and faith we can carry to others to also be successful in recovery through the Twelve Steps and through faith in Christ. And it is with this spiritual awakening we now have God in our life to help us day by day to practice these principles in all areas of our life.

The passage for today from John speaks about being born again, about being born again spiritually. The phrase "born again" simply means to bring God into your life by having faith in the Lord Jesus Christ. It expresses faith and an expression of trusting God with your life and not yourself or your own power. Being born again means you have had a spiritual awakening. The message of the Twelve Steps is a great message to share with others, because it is all about a spiritual awakening. Also, the message of the Twelve Steps is a great way of life because as we practice these steps day by day, we will stay focused on God and we will continually look to turn our will and our lives over to the care of God. I encourage you to continue growing in your spiritual awakening, to continue growing in your faith in God, and to continue on sharing this great message with others.

Prayer for today:

Dear Lord, thank you for the spiritual awakening of placing my faith and trust in you. Thank you for the great message that with faith in God I can be successful in recovery. Help me to continue to share this great message with other addicts and even all people everywhere.

Notes of gratitude, progress, concerns, and prayers for today:

____

____

____

____

____

____

____

____

Peace That Surpasses All Understanding

And the peace of God, which surpasses all understanding, will guard your hearts and your minds in Christ Jesus. (Philippians 4:7 ESV)

We are all made with a 'God sized hole' which many believe represents our inner desires of the heart for fulfillment, happiness, value, and meaning in life. These inner desires of the heart can only be filled by a relationship with God. That is how we are made and only a relationship with God can fill this 'God sized hole'. Unfortunately, we often seek to fill this hole with things outside of God, but they will always leave us lacking. We seek to fill this 'God sized hole' with alcohol, drugs, sex, money, success, power, physical beauty, but whatever we try, it is never enough. It seems whatever we seek to fill this hole is never enough and we think all we need is just a little bit more. If we just get a little bit more, then we will be "happy".

When we bring God into our life, we will change our focus. We will then focus on seeking to honor God with our life. It is with God that we will fill this 'God sized hole' and we will see that our life is dramatically different. We will have peace. One of the personal stories in *Alcoholics Anonymous* puts it this way:

> "So, as I have worked the program, I have grown emotionally and intellectually. I not only have peace *with* God, I have the peace *of* God through an active God consciousness. I have not only recovered from alcoholism, I have become whole in person—body, spirit, soul."[37]

Do you want peace in your life? Do you want to have peace in your mind, body, and spirit? As you bring God into your life and seek his will in your life, you can have peace. As the apostle Paul says in Philippians, you can have "the peace of God, which surpasses all understanding." When you go to bed and lay your head down at night you can have peace in your mind, body, and spirit and you will close your eyes with calmness and peace; the peace of God will fill your 'God sized hole' with a peace that surpasses all understanding.

Prayer for today:

Dear Lord, I pray for this peace. Please dear Lord come into my life and help me to focus on you and honoring you with my life. Thank you for a peace that surpasses all understanding.

Notes of gratitude, progress, concerns, and prayers for today:

____

____

____

____

____

____

____

____

____

____

Day 58 of 100

You Are a Child of God

See what great love the Father has lavished on us, that we should be called children of God! And that is what we are! (1 John 3:1 NIV)

Likely, one challenge you may have is to leave the past in the past. Often the life of addiction has lasted for many years and it has become the only way of life that you've known. Even more so, that may be how you see yourself today as an addict or alcoholic. It is important to remember you are an addict or alcoholic and that you cannot use drugs or drink alcohol and that your limit is zero. You cannot have even one and you cannot simply use softer drugs. Accepting and even embracing this as your new truth and your new way of life will actually be quite freeing. But, now you are not the same person as you were before when you were in your addiction. If you have brought God into your life with Step Three or at any other point, then your identity has changed dramatically. You are now a "child of God". It is important to remember that you are in recovery for sure, but you are a child of God in recovery.

It may be difficult to view yourself as a child of God, but that is exactly what the Bible says. You may not feel like a child of God, but faith and life and recovery are not always about how you feel. Our feelings will vary from moment to moment, but we need to rely on the truths of the Bible. We can trust what the Bible says and what it reveals about God. In fact, the Bible is the most common way that God reveals himself to us. We can trust the Bible to teach us and to show us more about God and his nature.

This verse today from 1 John 3:1 is an amazing passage that reveals God's great love for us and for you. As you read this passage, consider God is saying this about you personally. That God has such a great love for you, he calls you a child of God and that is what you are! This is a great passage that again reinforces the description of God as a loving, caring, and compassionate God. You are not perfect and you may have a terrible past, but God still loves you and even today calls you a child of God. I encourage you to embrace this great truth and to live each day more and more aware that you are a new person, that you are now a child of God.

Prayer for today:

Dear Lord, thank you for this great truth of the Bible that I am a child of God. Help me to understand this truth that frees me from the bondage of drugs and alcohol. I am a child of God and I leave my past in the past and embrace my new life in recovery as a child of God.

Notes of gratitude, progress, concerns, and prayers for today:

____

____

____

____

____

____

____

____

____

____

Day 59 of 100

Help My Unbelief

Jesus said to him, "If you can believe, all things are possible to him who believes." [24] ***Immediately the father of the child cried out and said with tears, "Lord, I believe; help my unbelief!"***
(Mark 9:23-24 NKJV)

One difficulty of coming back to the Lord is the shame and guilt we have from all of our years of turning away from God with reckless living. Many in addiction struggle with the overwhelming amount of shame and guilt they feel inside and they doubt God will take them back. They desperately want to come back to God and to receive his forgiveness, but they are not sure God will actually forgive them. Perhaps that is how you feel right now. Perhaps you feel what you have done in the past is just too terrible for God to really and truly forgive you. You have doubt. You doubt God. You want to believe, but you have doubt. *Alcoholics Anonymous* speaks to this:

> "If we are sorry for what we have done, and have the honest desire to let God take us to better things, we believe we will be forgiven."[38]

In essence, this quote means if you are sorry and have an honest desire to be forgiven, God will forgive you. The shame and guilt you feel is actually an appropriate response to where you are right now today and it shows you are beginning to feel your emotions again and you are beginning to see your condition before a holy God accurately. But, please understand God does not want you to stay in your shame and guilt. God wants you to confess your sins to him and then to accept his forgiveness.

But this may not be an easy step to take. You may indeed doubt God. You may feel while he will forgive others, you doubt he will forgive you. The passage today in the Gospel of Mark is a great passage for doubt and unbelief. A father has doubt that Jesus will heal is child and the father "cried out and said with tears, 'Lord, I believe; help my unbelief!'" I encourage you to cry out to God, perhaps even with tears, and ask God to help your unbelief. Please know God will help your unbelief and he will indeed forgive you. With God's forgiveness you can leave your shame and guilt in the past and allow God to move in your life. Trust God to answer your cry for help and to help your unbelief.

Prayer for today:

Dear Lord, you know my past and yet you promise to forgive me of all my sins and for that I am forever grateful. I ask you to help my unbelief and to help me trust you more and more each day.

Notes of gratitude, progress, concerns, and prayers for today:

____

____

____

____

____

____

____

____

____

____

Day 60 of 100

Every Day Is a Milestone

Fear not, for I am with you; Be not dismayed, for I am your God. I will strengthen you, Yes, I will help you, I will uphold you with My righteous right hand.
(Isaiah 41:10 NKJV)

Milestones are important. It is important for us to recognize recovery milestones at significant points in our recovery, ten days, thirty days, sixty days, ninety days, one year and so on. The addict and alcoholic are coming from a life so full of chaos and confusion; any return to order, consistency, and structure is a good thing and should be affirmed. As you consider your milestone for today, it gives you an opportunity to pause and to reflect back to how far you have come in recovery. Sixty days clean and sober is indeed a wonderful milestone to recognize (or whatever milestone you are at today). As you reflect back what changes can you see in your life over these past days in recovery? How long has it been since you were clean and sober for sixty days or for your personal time in recovery?

But, let me point out every day clean and sober is another great milestone! For those that are afflicted with addiction or alcoholism, it is indeed challenging every day to be clean and sober. Recovery is not easy, but it is possible when you take it one day at a time. This quote from *Alcoholics Anonymous* expresses the one day at a time approach and it is how days add up to many milestones in recovery.

> "The next question they asked was, 'You can quit twenty-four hours, can't you?' I said, 'Sure, yes, anybody can do that, for twenty-four hours.' They said, 'That's what we're talking about. Just twenty-four hours at a time.'"[39]

Recovery is not easy and you may be full of questions and doubts, but this passage from Isaiah encourages you to "Fear not". While you do not know what tomorrow holds this passage from the

Bible tells you to not be afraid and that God is with you! Do not be dismayed or troubled for God "will strengthen you" and He "will help you". These encouraging words remind us of our Higher Power, the God of our understanding, the God of the Bible will be with you and will help you and he will strengthen you! With God in your life and as you seek his will in your life, you can be clean and sober one more day and then tomorrow you can recognize another milestone day in recovery. Each and every day is a milestone!

Prayer for today:

Dear Lord, I am so grateful to be growing in my recovery but I am especially grateful for today, another day clean and sober. Thank you for your promise to strengthen me and to help me in my times of struggle.

Notes of gratitude, progress, concerns, and prayers for today:

____

____

____

____

____

____

____

____

____

____

Day 61 of 100

You Are a Conqueror

No, in all these things we are more than conquerors through him who loved us. (Romans 8:37 NIV)

For those in bondage to alcohol or drugs, you are all too aware you are in a battle. There is no easy switch or button to simply turn off your addiction. It is a battle. This quote from the *Alcoholics Anonymous* describes the battle in a brutally clear manner:

> "At this point I was in a vicious battle to control my drinking. I knew that if I took only one drink, I'd lose complete control and drink until I passed out. Nevertheless, I tried day after day to beat this obsession with alcohol.... (later at an AA meeting) I looked at the faces of the people in the room and I saw it. I saw the understanding, the empathy, the love. Today I believe I saw my Higher Power for the first time in those faces. While still up at the podium, it hit me—this is what I had been looking for all my life."[40]

This quote brings out several important truths for those in recovery. First, to understand you are in a battle! You are in a war and sometimes the war is a 'vicious battle' for your very life. Second, you cannot have even one drink or use even one time. The limit is zero. You cannot have even one. The third point that comes out is you can win the battle! You can be victorious and you can be a conqueror in your battle with addiction. Regardless of how many times you may have failed in the past, now with God in your life as your true Higher Power, you can be successful in recovery. God will do for you what you could not do for yourself.

This passage in Romans describes believers as being conquerors, and even more than conquerors. What a great description of what Christians are in Christ. We are conquerors. But, if we are conquerors, that means we are in a battle; it means we are in a fight for our lives and it won't be easy. But we are not in the battle alone; you are not in the battle alone! God is with you and he will bring others around you to help you. God will help you to have victory over your addiction. God will help you to be a conqueror. With God in your life you can be successful in recovery. I encourage you today to look to the loving God of the Bible as the true Higher Power. With God in your life you can be a conqueror over your battle with addiction and you can have that same feeling "this is what I had been looking for all my life."

Prayer for today:

Dear Lord, please continue to help me with my battle over my addiction. It is indeed a battle and I cannot do it alone, thank you for your help and strength.

Notes of gratitude, progress, concerns, and prayers for today:

____

____

____

____

____

____

____

____

____

____

Day 62 of 100

The Very Best You Can Be

Whatever you do, work at it with all your heart, as working for the Lord, not for human masters. (Colossians 3:23 NIV)

Every step along the way in your recovery is an important part of your recovery. As you progress forward in recovery, embrace each step and take full advantage of all the resources made available to you, whether a rehab facility, a recovery house, longer term recovery facility or even at home. Learn as much as you can at each phase and do everything you can to prepare yourself for the next step. When it comes time for you to leave and move on to the next phase of your recovery, you want to have the assurance you did everything possible to prepare yourself for that next step.

One step you will need to take at some point is to get a job again so you can pay the bills, but keep your recovery still priority number one. With recovery as your number one priority, you need to find a job that supports your continued success in recovery. That will probably mean your job at this point will not be a dream job, but will be the type of job that will enable you to continue making progress in recovery. God has gifted each of us with certain skills and abilities. It is important to be mindful of just how God has gifted you and then to use those skills and abilities in your job now and also in the future. Regardless of whatever job you have, be the very best employee you can be. Ultimately, every job we have is one that provides a service or product for people. God wants us to be the very best we can be in service to people, and ultimately our work is a way to honor God. When you go to work today, have the mindset to be the very best employee you can be, one that cares for people and one that seeks to honor God in your work.

The passage today from Colossians speaks of the same type of instruction even back in the New Testament times, to be the very best you can be. The apostle Paul was instructing the believers saying "Whatever you do, work at it with all your heart, as working for the

Lord." I encourage you to embrace this mindset and that today you would have the mindset to be the very best you can be in your job, in your recovery, and even in whatever you do!

Prayer for today:

Dear Lord, I thank you for blessing me with different skills and abilities. Help me to honor you in whatever I do whether in my job or service or even any interaction with people. Help me to serve others with all my heart as unto you.

Notes of gratitude, progress, concerns, and prayers for today:

____

____

____

____

____

____

____

____

____

____

Day 63 of 100

The Most Important Thing

Jesus replied: "'Love the Lord your God with all your heart and with all your soul and with all your mind.' [38] This is the first and greatest commandment. [39] And the second is like it: 'Love your neighbor as yourself.'" (Matthew 22:37-39 NIV)

As we ponder what is the most important thing in life, many will remember the two most important commandments to love God above all else and to love our neighbor as yourself. And these two commandments are indeed the most important, but for those in recovery, these commands are lived out in a dramatically different way. It is to stay clean and sober! Without being clean and sober, everything else in life falls apart and leads back to a life that would quickly become unmanageable. Being clean and sober is a way of loving God. The *Twenty-Four Hours a Day* book describes the utmost priority that sobriety should have when it states:

> "As long as I keep in mind that liquor can never be my friend again, but is now my deadly enemy, and as long as I remember that my main business is keeping sober and that it's the most important thing in my life I believe I'll be prepared for that crucial moment when the idea of having a drink pops into my mind."[41]

For those in recovery, the most important thing is to continue to be clean and sober and this is absolutely a way to love God and is also a way to love others. The quote above reflects a core principle of recovery to do everything necessary to be successful in recovery and that certainly includes the perspective that alcohol and drugs are not your friend, but a deadly enemy. You will face the temptation to drink or use again and, unfortunately, perhaps even hounded daily by that temptation, so it is absolutely critical you keep the perspective that drugs and alcohol are not your friend, but your enemy. This will help you be prepared to respond to that temptation in a way that will honor God.

In the passage today from Matthew, Jesus gives the simple declaration of the two most important commandments basically to love God and to love people. Everything else does flow from these two commandments. For those in recovery, this will mean to have the foremost focus on being clean and sober. But beyond that, for those in recovery and for all believers, love for God will go much deeper. As we grow closer to the Lord, we will understand more and more what it means to love God with all our heart, soul, and mind! I encourage you to continue to grow closer to the Lord and in your love for God. Continue to do whatever is necessary to be successful in recovery and continue to grow in your love for God and in your love for people and in that you will fulfill the two greatest commandments.

Prayer for today:

Dear Lord, you know my heart. You know that I love you, but you know my struggle as well. Help me to continue on in recovery as the first and foremost way I can love you. With your help I can be successful in recovery.

Notes of gratitude, progress, concerns, and prayers for today:

____

____

____

____

____

____

Day 64 of 100

Not Perfect - But Forgiven

My dear children, I write this to you so that you will not sin. But if anybody does sin, we have an advocate with the Father—Jesus Christ, the Righteous One. (1 John 2:1 NIV)

The Bible says we become a Christian by grace through faith in the Lord Jesus Christ. Once we take that step of faith and put our trust in the Lord Jesus, that fact will never change. All of our past sins will be wiped away. All the sins of our addiction, the times we hurt others, the times we lied or stole, the times we rejected God, these sins will be forgiven and washed away as white as snow. In that instant, we will become a child of God and that will never change. We will always be a Christian. We will always be a believer. However, there may be times we question whether we really are Christians. We may have doubts about our relationship with God because we do not feel the same way as we did when we first brought God into our life. It is important to understand just because we become a Christian that does not mean we will be perfect. It does not mean we will no longer sin. Unfortunately, we will sometimes still sin. But, one way that we can have assurance we are a Christian and our faith is true and real is how we feel when we do sin. As a believer, when we do sin we feel remorse. We feel like we let God down and we have the natural inclination to seek forgiveness.

This passage today in 1 John 2 is a comforting passage that talks about this very thing. God understands we are flawed human beings and there will be times we will still sin and fall short of God's will for us. But, this passage reassures us "if anybody does sin, we have an advocate with the Father—Jesus Christ, the Righteous One." What an amazing verse. God does not expect perfection, and he even provides forgiveness when we fail him. But, our life should reflect progress. This progress is a life that seeks to gradually be transformed into a life that honors God. And when we do sin we can confess our sins to God because "we have an advocate with the Father".

Whenever you do sin consider these four simple steps in response.

1) Acknowledge your sin before God and ask God for his forgiveness.
2) Humbly accept God's forgiveness and do not dwell in the remorse of your sin.
3) Take whatever practical steps are necessary so you will not fall into that sin again.
4) Move on from your sin and be open to God moving in your life again even today.

Leave your past in the past. I encourage you to seek to grow in your relationship with God and to remember that you are not perfect, but you are forgiven.

Prayer for today:

Dear Lord, I thank you for your forgiveness to me a humble and grateful failed human being. Help me to grow closer and closer to you and for me to honor you with my life and actions.

Notes of gratitude, progress, concerns, and prayers for today:

____

____

____

____

____

____

____

Day 65 of 100

A Brand New Power

But Jesus looked at them and said, "With man this is impossible, but with God all things are possible."
(Matthew 19:26 ESV)

The grips of addiction are devastating. In the times you have a clear mind you know you should stop, you know you want to stop, but you cannot stop no matter how hard you try. You look desperately for the right rehab facility that will help you make it in recovery. You look for the right counselor, the right sponsor, the right mentor or friend, but all have failed. You try countless books and even many meetings, but all have failed and leave you still in bondage to your addiction. Regardless of how hard you try in your own power, you always fall back into addiction and you fall even harder and deeper each time.

You need a new and dramatically different approach. You need a new power, a brand new power. *Alcoholics Anonymous* speaks to this new power:

> "Lack of power, that was our dilemma. We had to find a power by which we could live, and it had to be *a Power greater than ourselves*. Obviously. But where and how were we to find this Power? Well, that's exactly what this book is about....That means we have written a book which we believe to be spiritual as well as moral. And it means, of course, that we are going to talk about God."[42]

If you have tried everything else, consider that God could be the brand new power you have been seeking. I encourage you to bring God into your life. Trust there is a God in heaven, who is the creator of the entire world. Trust he is a loving, caring, and compassionate God, and he wants to help you be successful in recovery. The bondage of addiction is relentless and to break free of that bondage takes a brand new power.

In the passage today from Matthew, Jesus speaks to the disciples, telling them of the power that is needed for salvation, for freedom from the bondage of sin. Jesus tells the disciples that on their own it is impossible, but "with God all things are possible." On your own, it is impossible to be free from the bondage of your addiction, but you have access to a power greater than yourself. You have access to a brand new power by bringing God into your life. Just as in this passage, Jesus is looking at you today and is saying the same message to you "With man this is impossible, but with God all things are possible." I encourage you today to accept this message and bring God into your life and accept this brand new power. With God in your life and with this brand new power of God, a power greater than yourself, you can be successful in recovery.

Prayer for today:

Dear Lord, I recognize that I absolutely need a power greater than myself. I ask you to come into my life and to be this brand new power; with you in my life I can be successful in recovery.

Notes of gratitude, progress, concerns, and prayers for today:

____

____

____

____

____

____

____

Day 66 of 100

Wait for the Roller Coaster to Stop

Lead me in your truth and teach me, for you are the God of my salvation; for you I wait all the day long. (Psalm 25:5 ESV)

Making the decision to do whatever is necessary to be successful in recovery is a tremendous step to take and most likely a lifesaving decision. It is absolutely the right decision to make and you and your loved ones will be blessed beyond measure for making this dramatic decision to do whatever is necessary to be successful in recovery. But, in early recovery, it is important to understand in many ways you are on a roller coaster. You will probably have a flood of emotions, anxiety, guilt, and doubt all combined with many life changes. *Alcoholics Anonymous* describes this situation as:

> "Sobriety is nothing like I thought it would be. At first it was one big emotional roller coaster, full of sharp highs and deep lows. My emotions were new, untested, and I wasn't entirely certain I wanted to deal with them. I cried when I should have been laughing. I laughed when I should have cried. Events I thought were the end of the world turned out to be gifts. It was all very confusing. Slowly things began to even out. As I began to take the steps of recovery, my role in the pitiful condition of my life became clear."[43]

It is important to remember in early recovery you are going through many dramatic changes and it will take time for you to heal in many ways including physically, spiritually, emotionally, and medically. It is also important you give yourself time to heal before making any big decisions in your life. This includes making any significant relationship decisions. *Alcoholics Anonymous* and *Narcotics Anonymous* both indicate the importance of waiting before making any relationship decisions while in early recovery. The guideline is often stated to wait one year in recovery before making any significant relationship decisions. Be patient and establish a firm recovery foundation before making any significant relationship or life decisions. Are you willing to do whatever is necessary to be successful in recovery, even if it means waiting to make any relationship decisions?

Psalm 25:5 reminds us we have so much to learn, so much for God to teach us. Wherever you are at in your recovery, I encourage you to learn everything you can right now during this time in recovery. Learn all you can to help prepare you for the next step in recovery and in life. As you seek God and his truth, he will prepare you for life and prepare you for making any relationship decisions, as you wait on his will in your life. As you seek God, be open for God to lead you in his truth and to teach you so that you will be prepared to do whatever is necessary to be successful in recovery.

Prayer for today:

Dear Lord, help me to understand that I have so much healing needed and so much to learn about you and your will in my life. Help me to be patient and to wait on your clear direction in my life for any significant changes.

Notes of gratitude, progress, concerns, and prayers for today:

____

____

____

____

____

____

Day 67 of 100

No Matter What – Trust God

Trust in the Lord with all your heart, And lean not on your own understanding;[6] In all your ways acknowledge Him, And He shall direct your paths.
(Proverbs 3:5-6 NKJV)

Recovery is not easy; it is probably the hardest thing you will ever do. But, while it is not easy in many ways it is simple. The simple basic strategy of recovery is don't use and don't drink. Don't pick up and don't drink, everything else gets better after that. Yes, this is a simple rule, but we all know it is terribly difficult. It is terribly difficult to do on your own, but you do not need to do it on your own. The books of *Alcoholics Anonymous* and *Narcotics Anonymous* both speak about a personal spiritual experience with your higher power. As you make this personal decision to surrender your life and will to the care of God, he will help you through any and every situation. *Narcotics Anonymous* describes it as:

> "I don't have to rob and steal to make ends meet. I am no longer standing on street corners waiting for the man to turn up. I don't have cops busting my door, and I have this unshakable faith that all will be well, no matter what happens, as long as I don't pick up, I go to meetings, and I trust my higher power."[44]

No matter what happens, don't pick up, don't drink and trust God. It will not be easy, but God will help you get through those times you fear you will not be able to get past. Continue to surround yourself with other individuals that share your desire to be clean and sober and also share your love for God. When you are struggling, pray and trust God and He will meet your need, perhaps with someone to help you get past your struggle and get safely to the other side.

The passage today from Proverbs instructs us to put our faith and trust in the Lord God of heaven. Not just a casual hope or wish, but to trust God with our whole heart. Trust God with everything we have! We are not to look to our own understanding, or our own thoughts, or our own plans, as they have failed us in the past. This day and every day, no matter what happens, put your faith and trust in the Lord God with your whole heart. Begin each day with a prayer and ask God to help you go one more day clean and sober. One thing you can be sure of is bad times will come. You will struggle again and you will at some point be tempted to use or to drink again. For those times, stop and say a prayer again and ask God to help you, so no matter what happens, you will not pick up or drink. Do whatever is necessary to be successful in recovery. You can trust God to help you. Pray every day so no matter what happens, you will trust God with your whole heart and you will end another day clean and sober and successful in recovery.

Prayer for today:

Dear Lord, thank you so much for your promise to direct my paths. Help me to have the courage to follow your paths. I pray each day for you to help me trust you more and to trust you with all of my heart.

Notes of gratitude, progress, concerns, and prayers for today:

____

____

____

____

____

Be Honest with Yourself and Others

Do not lie to each other, since you have taken off your old self with its practices [10] and have put on the new self, which is being renewed in knowledge in the image of its Creator. (Colossians 3:9-10 NIV)

One of the common failings of addicts is not being honest. Often addicts are not honest with themselves and they are not honest with others. The life of the addict may at times continue to build lie upon lie even when it is really not necessary, but lying somehow becomes an integral part of life. Dishonesty then just leads to even more troubles and, unfortunately, would often lead towards continued addiction or towards a relapse. In addition, the addict will feel even more undeserving and unworthy because deep down inside, they will acknowledge that they are living a lie. The *Alcoholics Anonymous* states:

> "More than most people, the alcoholic leads a double life. He is very much the actor. To the outer world he presents his stage character. This is the one he likes his fellows to see. He wants to enjoy a certain reputation, but knows in his heart he doesn't deserve it."[45]

The passage today from Colossians speaks of putting off the old self and putting on and embracing the new self. The old self would lie and be full of dishonesty to get whatever was needed for another drink or drug or to tell the right story, but the new self is being renewed! As you bring God into your life and make the decision to turn your life and your will over to the care of God, you are being renewed in to a brand new self. You are being renewed in to the image of God. You are being renewed by a loving, caring, compassionate, and merciful God who loves you and wants to help you. The instruction in this passage is "do not lie to each other" and to "put on the new self" and this new self is being transformed into the image of God. What an amazing truth of God and of Scripture!

I challenge you to begin today to be honest with yourself and with others. Be honest with yourself and others in a loving and caring way and not in a harsh or mean-spirited way. Begin even today and see what God can do in your life. Embrace honesty, embrace truth, and embrace the opportunity of God moving in your life to change you in a dramatic way! This transformation will not be quick, it will be gradual. But, with God's help, you can be transformed from your "old self" and renewed into your brand "new self", one who is renewed in the image of God.

Prayer for today:

Dear Lord, I am so grateful that you are renewing me in to the image of God. Help me to be honest to myself, to others, and to you and thank you for the freedom to finally be honest.

Notes of gratitude, progress, concerns, and prayers for today:

____

____

____

____

____

____

____

____

____

Day 69 of 100

Recognize Milestones of Life

Forget the former things; do not dwell on the past. [19] See, I am doing a new thing! Now it springs up; do you not perceive it? I am making a way in the wilderness and streams in the wasteland.
(Isaiah 43:18-19 NIV)

We recently recognized a member of our recovery group who celebrated 33 years sober. It was not a big celebration, but a grateful recognition of 33 years of doing the next right thing. This dear woman has continued to be a wonderful support and encouragement to many in our group, to many in our recovery community, and even to many throughout our local community. It is important to seek ways to offer support, encouragement, and service to others, as that action alone does indeed help many people and it also helps each of us as we look to support, encourage, and help others. Helping others takes the focus off of us and onto helping others, and that is a wonderful thing indeed.

It is also important to be mindful of milestones in our life, such as 33 years sober or perhaps 30 days, one year, or even just one more day clean and sober. These milestones indicate change. They are concrete evidence of a new way of living and of the dramatic work God is doing in our life. Do not minimize these milestones as they do indicate the amazing blessing and work of God in our lives. By recognizing and celebrating these milestones it helps us understand better just how far we have come and how much change is really taking place in our lives and it reveals just how much God is doing in our lives.

The passage today from Isaiah instructs us to "Forget the former things" and to "not dwell on the past", because God is "doing a new thing". What wonderful words of instruction! Do not dwell in the past, but be mindful and grateful of all the new things that God is doing now. I encourage you today to reflect on how far God has brought you in recovery and to be grateful for all that God is doing in your life today. Whether your time in recovery is short or long, I encourage you to be grateful you have another opportunity in recovery and to remember God is doing a "new thing" in your life. Embrace this recovery milestone, whatever it might be, and remember, God is not done yet "doing a new thing" in your life.

Prayer for today:

Dear Lord thank you for another chance at life. Help me to honor you with this new opportunity at life starting even this very day.

Notes of gratitude, progress, concerns, and prayers for today:

____

____

____

____

____

____

____

____

____

Day 70 of 100

Keep Coming Back

So he got up and went to his father. "But while he was still a long way off, his father saw him and was filled with compassion for him; he ran to his son, threw his arms around him and kissed him.... Let's have a feast and celebrate. [24] For this son of mine was dead and is alive again; he was lost and is found."
(Luke 15:20-24 NIV)

Recovery is not easy and sometimes individuals in recovery are unsuccessful the first time. For some, recovery may include a relapse. It is encouraging to hear stories of individuals that are successful in recovery for years and even decades, but sometimes when you hear these stories, they may include one or more relapses. Each time in recovery, learning from the past and changing what needs to be changed. As has been said elsewhere in this devotional, 'if nothing changes, then nothing changes'. It is absolutely important to learn from the past failures and honestly make whatever changes are necessary to be successful in recovery. Be committed to do whatever is necessary to be successful in recovery. And the most important thing is to keep coming back! Regardless of how many times you may fail, keep coming back. Come back to your recovery groups and most importantly, keep coming back to God. Keep coming back to God and ask for his forgiveness and help again.

The passage today is from Luke 15, from the story of the "prodigal son" or sometimes called the "lost son". The passage is relevant for each of us in some way, and certainly many in recovery can relate to this story as well. Read the full story from Luke 15:11-32. It is quite dramatic and revealing how God has deep compassion for each of us. It is especially significant that it is Jesus who is telling this story, and he wants us to be clear this is how God the father will respond to each of us when we come back to him. The son eventually goes back to his father and confesses his wrongs and simply asks to be a servant for his father, but the father is "filled with compassion for him" and he "ran to his son" and "threw his arms around him". What a beautiful picture of a compassionate father! And Jesus wants us to understand this is how our heavenly father will respond to us when we come back to him.

Regardless of what you have done in the past, keep coming back to God. Confess your sins and come back to God. Learn from the past, accept God's forgiveness, and continue to start a new journey with God in your life. As this story describes, God is longing for you to come back to him and he is eager to forgive you and to have a restored relationship with you again. No matter what happens, leave the past in the past and keep coming back to God.

Prayer for today:

Dear Lord, thank you for this beautiful model of compassion and for the message that you simply want us to come back to you. Help me to leave my past in the past and to come back to you for a brand new start.

Notes of gratitude, progress, concerns, and prayers for today:

____

____

____

____

____

____

____

____

Day 71 of 100

Embrace Today

This is the day that the Lord has made;
let us rejoice and be glad in it.
(Psalm 118:24 ESV)

Regardless of where you are at in your recovery and in your life circumstances, it is likely you face many challenges and tough decisions. Often we look at the struggles we are in the midst of right now today and we feel that once we get past these immediate challenges, then "things" will be better. We convince ourselves once we get past ninety days clean and sober, or once we get a new job, or once we get a new apartment, or once we get our fines paid, or once we get our medical issues resolved, or many other circumstances then we will be "better" and then we will be "happy". To this point author John Ortberg states:

> "We all live with the illusion that joy will come someday when conditions change....If we are going to rejoice, it must be in this day. This is the day that the Lord has made."[46]

The first implication is that we will be happy and joyful someday, but only when our conditions change. Certainly, it is important to carefully consider the many issues and struggles we each face and to make wise decisions. But I encourage you to not be so overwhelmed with tomorrow that you neglect today. Do not skip today merely because you have issues and struggles. I suggest to you we will always have issues and struggles in some manner. If you woke up today and you are still alive, then God is not done with you yet! Be grateful and even joyful for another day of life and another opportunity to be successful in recovery. Yes, there are challenges and struggles, but there will always be challenges to some extent. The key is to remember we do not face them alone; God is with us and will help us. Any challenge you face, you can face knowing God will help you through any and every situation and for that great biblical truth, you can be joyful.

The passage today from Psalm 118 is the simple message today is the day the Lord has made and we can be joyful in it. Embrace today and be joyful, and do not skip over today! Be open and mindful of what God is doing in your life even today and be joyful. Even in the midst of challenges, you can be joyful because you know God is with you and will help you. Embrace today and be joyful in all God is doing in your life, even today.

Prayer for today:

Dear Lord, thank you for another day of life! Help me to not look past today and help me to be joyful even in today. You are a great God and I look forward to what you have for me today.

Notes of gratitude, progress, concerns, and prayers for today:

____

____

____

____

____

____

____

____

____

____

Are You Dancing with the Devil?

Do not be deceived: "Bad company ruins good morals." (1 Corinthians 15:33 ESV)

At a recovery meeting one evening, the speaker was talking about the victim mindset and she mentioned a quote from Steve Maraboli where he states "the victim mindset will have you dancing with the devil, then complaining you're in hell."[47] This is a great insight and a great description of the life of an addict and alcoholic. For the addict, if you continue to live a life with no regard for God and continue to run with reckless and abusive people, then it really will not be surprising your life is full of trouble and chaos. This devotional book advocates the recovery principle to surround yourself with people that share your desire to be clean and sober and also share your love for God. But, the "dancing with the devil" quote is the opposite of this recovery principle; meaning if you surround yourself with people that drink and use drugs and reject God, that will also affect you and will simply pull you down and ultimately bring you to destruction.

The passage for today from 1 Corinthians 15:33 is an excellent passage and again it reveals to us God understands us and knows us inside and out. This verse is more evidence the Bible is a divinely inspired book and a book that was written by the God of heaven who made each of us and who understands us. This verse encourages us to "not be deceived" because it is important who we spend time with. It is important who our friends are, and it is important because the people we spend time with will affect us. Over time, the people we spend time with will influence us. The instruction that "Bad company ruins good morals" was true 2000 years ago, and it is still true today. This instruction is true for all people, but it is especially true for those in early recovery. It is so important for you to protect yourself from people, places, and things that might lead you to relapse. Protect yourself. Be wise and be cautious. Also, as you surround yourself with 'good company' and godly people that will influence you and will tend to 'build good morals' and strengthen your character. I encourage you today to reflect on who you spend time with. Begin today to be intentional to surround yourself with people that share your desire to be clean and sober and share your love for God.

Prayer for today:

Dear Lord, help me to be intentional and thoughtful of the individuals I spend time with. Give me wisdom to nurture friendships with people that share my desire to be clean and sober and that also share my love for you.

Notes of gratitude, progress, concerns, and prayers for today:

____

____

____

____

____

____

____

____

____

____

Day 73 of 100

Not My Will

Father, if you are willing, take this cup from me; yet not my will, but yours be done. (Luke 22:42 NIV)

So often we pray to God, asking for his intervention in our lives as if we know what is best for us. Whatever struggle or obstacle we are facing, we pray with specific requests that we see as the best scenario for us and we think that certainly God would see it our way too. But, if we reflect on the past our track record is not good. It is likely because of our past terrible decisions that led us into a life of addiction in the first place. Our focus is all wrong. Our focus should not be on ourselves and what is best or easiest for us, but our focus should be on what honors God. Simply our focus should be on seeking God's will in our life and the courage to be obedient. This is such a key component of recovery, and of life in general, that Step Three of the recovery stresses this very point "We made a decision to turn our will and our lives over to the care of God."[48] It is a way of thinking that is opposite of what we may naturally think. It may well be we are praying for the upcoming court decision to keep us out of prison, but that may be just the place God wants us to be. Prison may be best for our recovery or perhaps there are other lessons we need to learn or people we need to help while there. Certainly, God wants us to pray and to pray for specific requests, but we need to also pray for God's will whatever that might be, and then we need to be obedient.

The passage today from Luke 22 describes how Jesus prayed as he was facing his most difficult circumstance of his earthly life. Jesus was soon to be arrested and then crucified on the cross in a most brutal and painful death. His prayer was an honest prayer reflecting his humanity when he asked "if you are willing, take this cup from me." But, Jesus did not stop there he added "yet not my will, but yours be done." Jesus knew that his purpose in coming to earth was for this very reason, to pay the price on the cross for the sins of the world. He prayed an honest prayer and yet was fully yielding to the will of the Father. I encourage you to absolutely pray for specific requests with the mindset of seeking God's will in your life and to add to your prayer "yet not my will, but yours be done." Be open to however God might answer your prayer. God sees the big picture of your life and he knows what is best for you and he knows what he is preparing you for in the future. Have the courage to pray "not my will, but yours be done" and be mindful that God is preparing you for something in the future. You need to be prepared and ready for however God might use you in the future, as you are obedient to him and his will in your life.

Prayer for today:

Dear Lord, help me to keep your will foremost in my prayers and in my everyday actions of life. I thank you for answering my prayers. Help me to remember that you know what is best for me and help me to be obedient to your will in my life.

Notes of gratitude, progress, concerns, and prayers for today:

____

____

____

____

____

____

____

____

____

Day 74 of 100

You Are Doing a Great Work

And I sent messengers to them, saying, "I am doing a great work and I cannot come down. Why should the work stop while I leave it and come down to you?" (Nehemiah 6:3 ESV)

It is so easy to get distracted in recovery. Often it happens at some point in recovery you feel you have made it and you can stop doing some things you have been doing to be successful in recovery. Perhaps you feel you can stop going to meetings, or stop going to church, or stop doing service work, or stop going to faith-based meetings. There may even be times you feel you can start to drink just a little bit at dinner or perhaps start to use softer drugs and somehow feel that will not negatively affect your recovery. For addicts and alcoholics, it is important to remember everything you value in life depends on being successful in recovery. If you relapse, it will likely put everything else you value in jeopardy, perhaps even put your very life at risk. One more relapse could absolutely be the last and fatal one. Your very life does indeed depend on being successful in recovery.

Your recovery must come as priority number one for you, because if you are not successful in recovery, nothing else matters. Everything else will come falling down. There will be many people that will try to pull you away from your recovery. Perhaps some will have bad motives and yet perhaps others will have good intentions and will try to pull you away from your recovery for other seemingly worthy and noble reasons. But, only you can truly know what steps, actions, meetings, events, and boundaries are necessary for your recovery and you need to be firm to the commitment you made to yourself, your family, and loved ones when you committed to do everything necessary to be successful in recovery.

Much like the passage today from Nehemiah, and his work to rebuild the wall, your recovery is indeed "a great work". Your recovery is an ongoing work that will be for life and one you "cannot come down" from. But this great work of recovery enables you to be diligent and faithful to God's calling in your life. God has created you with a plan and a purpose for your life, but you need to be successful in recovery to be 'doing the great work' for which God has called you. Your recovery is priority number one, but that simply enables you to be active and engaged in your ultimate "great work", which is the plan and purpose God has for you. Continue your "great work" of recovery and I encourage you to consider the ultimate plan and purpose for which God has called you. Be diligent and faithful and continue on in your recovery and with the ultimate "great work" of God's plan and purpose in your life.

Prayer for today:

Dear Lord, thank you that you have a plan and purpose for me. Help me to keep my recovery as priority number one and help me to be diligent and faithful with the ultimate "great work" that you have for me beyond recovery.

Notes of gratitude, progress, concerns, and prayers for today:

____

____

____

____

____

____

____

____

Day 75 of 100

When in Doubt Turn to God

After this many of his disciples turned back and no longer walked with him. [67] So Jesus said to the twelve, "Do you want to go away as well?" [68] Simon Peter answered him, "Lord, to whom shall we go? You have the words of eternal life." (John 6:66-68 ESV)

As you progress through your recovery, it is important to get wise counsel from individuals you trust and value. Seek out individuals that will tell you the truth and not just what you might want to hear. Certainly, it is valuable to seek guidance from individuals that are already successful in recovery and to learn from their past experiences and to consider how their path of recovery might provide insights to you and your recovery. As you know, it is not easy to be successful in recovery. There will be times you feel like it is too difficult, too hard, too full of uncertainty, and perhaps just too overwhelming you are not sure you can continue. When these feelings of uncertainty and doubt come and you actually consider turning back and giving up on your recovery it is then that I encourage you to turn back to God. Draw even closer to God then before and ask him to direct you to the trusted and valued people in your recovery group and simply ask for help.

In the passage today from John, the people were troubled by a difficult teaching of Jesus and some actually turned back and no longer followed Jesus. The teaching was too difficult, too hard, and they simply did not understand Jesus was speaking of the spiritual perspective and not the physical. At that point, Jesus asked the disciples the simple question "Do you want to go away as well?" Then Simon Peter responded for the group and said "Lord, to whom shall we go? You have the words of eternal life." As you consider your struggles in recovery and when doubts come, I encourage you to remember this response from the apostle Peter "Lord, to whom shall we go? You have the words of eternal life." The Lord does indeed have the words of eternal life and the help for your recovery as well.

When struggles come or doubts come, turn to God and to God's Word, for the Bible does have "the words of eternal life". He will help you through any struggle in your recovery and even any struggle of life. He will bring just the right person to come along side you to help you through your struggle. When difficult times come I encourage you to turn to God and he will indeed help you through any and every struggle of life.

Prayer for today:

Dear Lord, I thank you that you have given us "the words of eternal life" in the Bible. Help me to daily read your Word so I can learn more about you. Help me to always remember that when difficult times come I can always turn to you.

Notes of gratitude, progress, concerns, and prayers for today:

____

____

____

____

____

____

____

____

____

____

Day 76 of 100

God Has a Plan for You

The word of the Lord came to me, saying,
[5] "Before I formed you in the womb I knew you,
before you were born I set you apart;
I appointed you as a prophet to the nations."
(Jeremiah 1:4-5 NIV)

A speaker one evening at our recovery meeting made a rather bold statement saying that he did not know what plan God had for anyone there, but he knew what God's plan was not for them. It was not God's plan for anyone there to be an addict and to die in their addiction. This was a rather blunt statement and got everyone's attention. While it is certainly true God can use any situation for good and God can use individuals in recovery in mighty ways to reach out and help others from their own struggle, the point of this statement is that God does not want anyone to become an addict and die in their addiction. That is not God's plan. But God can rescue us out of our addiction and he can turn our terrible past of addiction around and use our past to help others and even to honor God.

The passage today tells of the word of the Lord coming to Jeremiah and telling him how God formed him in the womb and he was set apart even while yet in his mother's womb. The passage goes even further and says God had appointed him as a prophet to the nations even before he was born. What an amazing story and an amazing truth of the prophet Jeremiah! Jeremiah went on to be a great prophet of God and a leader of the Old Testament. Now consider for yourself God formed you in the womb and God set you apart and even more, God had appointed you for a particular purpose even before you were yet born. That is also an amazing story and an amazing truth for you as well. While you may not feel like it right now, God formed you in the womb and set you apart for a particular purpose. You are indeed special to God and he loves you and wants you to be free of your bondage to drugs and alcohol so you can pursue the true purpose and plan God has for you. You are divinely created by a loving, caring, compassionate, and merciful God and he wants to help you be free of your bondage. Trust God and believe the truth that God formed you in the womb and he does indeed have a plan and purpose for you. I encourage you to continue in your recovery and to grow closer to God and he will gradually reveal more and more of his plan and purpose for you. Consider what plan God might be preparing you for later in life. Trust God and his plan for you and your future will be very different from your past.

Prayer for today:

Dear Lord, I am so grateful that you do have a plan and purpose for my life. Help me to do everything I can today to be prepared for what you have for me.

Notes of gratitude, progress, concerns, and prayers for today:

____

____

____

____

____

____

____

____

____

____

Day 77 of 100

Progress Not Perfection

Not that I have already obtained this or am already perfect, but I press on to make it my own, because Christ Jesus has made me his own.... But one thing I do: forgetting what lies behind and straining forward to what lies ahead. (Philippians 3:12-13 ESV)

We all tend to hurry. We want things to go faster. We want things now. We want to take shortcuts. We want to jump ahead. These are common feelings and often that is how we feel about recovery, we want it to go faster. If we have 30 days clean, we can't wait till we have 60 days, if we have 6 months we can't wait till we have 1 year. It is important to understand recovery is not a destination, but a journey. While you will not be perfect, it is important you are moving in the right direction, that you are making progress. As you continue making progress, you will see you are making different decisions than you did in the past. You are making progress, you are being transformed. Also, at each stage of your recovery, and of your walk with the Lord, God is teaching you important lessons. At each stage, there are principles and life lessons God wants you to learn so you are better prepared for your next step of recovery. It is important you learn everything you are supposed to learn at each stage of your recovery so you will be fully prepared for the next step. Take full advantage of all the meetings, counseling sessions, medical help, therapy, and spiritual growth, so you will be prepared to continue making progress in recovery.

The passage today from Philippians, the apostle Paul, speaks to this very point. Paul states directly as far as perfection he has not "already obtained this" and he is not "already perfect". He understands the Christian life is not about perfection here on earth, but it is about continuing to press on toward the goal. Growth in our faith and in our recovery takes time. It is not fast. The Christian life and recovery are about progress, not perfection. Paul also states another key principle "forgetting what lies behind and straining forward to what lies ahead." It is important to leave the past in the past. We have all done terrible things in our past, things we wish we could forget. We cannot change the past, but we can change the future. Holding on to the past will prevent us from making progress. But, what a great opportunity we each have. We cannot change the past but we have a new opportunity to change our future. Consider progress and not perfection. I encourage you to not skip any steps and to learn everything you are supposed to learn today so you can continue making progress. Embrace this new opportunity to be the man or woman God wants you to be. In your faith and in your recovery, continue pursuing progress, not perfection.

Prayer for today:

Dear Lord, help me to not take any shortcuts, but to take full advantage of every stage of my recovery. Help me to learn everything I am to learn today to prepare me for my next step in recovery.

Notes of gratitude, progress, concerns, and prayers for today:

____

____

____

____

____

____

____

____

Day 78 of 100

Do the Next Right Thing

No, O people, the Lord has told you what is good,
and this is what he requires of you:
to do what is right, to love mercy,
and to walk humbly with your God.
(Micah 6:8 NLT)

Sometimes we complicate things. We complicate life and we complicate our recovery. In recovery, we face many decisions and actions regarding the next steps to take for our recovery. What often happens is we are too focused on what we want and what we think is "best" for our recovery instead of calmly and with a clear mind asking God what he would have us do next. As we seek God's guidance and direction, he will bring wise godly individuals into our lives to give us wise counsel. It is important not to rush into any decision and to honestly pray and have thorough discussions with the godly individuals God has brought into our lives for this very reason, to give us wise counsel. It is important we at least hear them out and actually consider their guidance. The next right thing for us might not be what we first thought was the "best" thing for us, but as we pray, God will show us what he has for us as the next right thing.

The passage today from Micah speaks of basic instructions of life for us from God; and what he requires of us first is to calmly and with a clear mind consider to "do what is right". When we consider any situation of life and calmly and prayerfully ask God what he wants us to do, the answer will usually be rather clear. God wants us to "do the next right thing." Is the next right thing to use only softer drugs, or to buy only a six-pack of beer, or to skip your group meeting, or to have casual sex, or to leave the rehab facility early, or to have daily devotions, or to go to work? When we prayerfully and honestly consider any situation of life, the answer will usually be clear, God wants us to "do the next right thing." As you continue on each day doing the next right thing, this will begin to affect you. You will draw closer to God and you will begin to be more transformed into a godly person, the type of person God designed you to be. You will begin to show love and mercy to others. You will become more inclined to reach out and help others in need, responding in mercy and kindness. You will sense the blessing of walking "humbly with your God". Doing the next right thing will be a blessing to you, to your loved ones, and will be the right thing before God. I encourage you today to not over complicate your recovery or your life, but to prayerfully consider for yourself and your situation and simply "do the next right thing".

Prayer for today:

Dear Lord, thank you for your instruction to simply "do what is right". Today, help me to do the next right thing and to walk humbly with you.

Notes of gratitude, progress, concerns, and prayers for today:

____

____

____

____

____

____

____

____

____

What Do You See?

Suddenly there was such a violent earthquake that the foundations of the prison were shaken. At once all the prison doors flew open, and everyone's chains came loose. [27] The jailer woke up, and when he saw the prison doors open, he drew his sword and was about to kill himself because he thought the prisoners had escaped.
(Acts 16:26-27 NIV)

After years of drugs and alcohol, our lives can become pretty devastated. Likely our physical and mental health will be terrible, our financial situation close to bankrupt, our relationships may be nearly destroyed, our job history full of short stays over many years, our police record may be quite long, and we may wonder can our lives ever be repaired or is it too late? Your life circumstances may be so damaged you may wonder can your life ever be restored. Is there any hope? If you attend recovery meetings then you already know most addicts get to this "bottom" at some point in their life and they will often share of a dramatic and miraculous change in their life. They will share that at just the right time, God rescued them. When they responded to this gift of desperation and turned to God with a commitment as never before they found God was still there and God rescued them. Despite how bad their life circumstances might have looked at the time, with God, there is always hope. God can dramatically intervene in ways we cannot even imagine. God is still in the miracle business as we turn to him and put our hope and trust in him and not in ourselves.

The passage today from Acts 16 is a portion of the story of Paul and Silas unjustly put in prison and bound with chains, and the prison guard was given strict orders to watch them closely. After a violent earthquake, the prison doors were opened and the chains all came loose. The jailer woke up and saw the prison doors open and to him, it looked like all the prisoners had escaped. He thought there was no hope for him. From what he could see with his own eyes and his own understanding, he thought all the prisoners had escaped and that would mean certain death for him and so he was about to kill himself. From all he could see, his life was over. However, the rest of the passage reads: "[28] But Paul shouted, "Don't harm yourself! We are all here!" [29] The jailer called for lights, rushed in and fell trembling before Paul and Silas. [30] He then brought them out and asked, "Sirs, what must I do to be saved?" [31] They replied, "Believe in the Lord Jesus, and you will be saved."

God intervened in his life in a way he could not see as possible. No matter how terrible things may look for you right now, no situation is beyond the reach of God. There is always hope with God. Put your hope and trust in God for a miracle or strength and courage through the struggle.

Prayer for today:

Dear Lord, I am so grateful that you still perform miracles and I know you have saved my life many times already. Help me to put my hope and trust in you. I know that regardless of what my situation looks like you can intervene in a mighty way.

Notes of gratitude, progress, concerns, and prayers for today:

____

____

____

____

____

____

____

Day 80 of 100

Let Go and Let God

Be anxious for nothing, but in everything by prayer and supplication, with thanksgiving, let your requests be made known to God; [7] and the peace of God, which surpasses all understanding, will guard your hearts and minds through Christ Jesus.
(Philippians 4:6-7 NKJV)

Life is complicated and the life of an addict is even more complicated and full of so many difficult life circumstances, it can easily feel overwhelming. Perhaps that is how you feel right now that you have so many issues, struggles, decisions, and dilemmas you do not know where to start. Likely, this is not the first time you felt this way, but as you reflect on the past times and your responses of the past, it is clear they did not work. Whatever you tried in the past failed and you are now left again to consider how to respond to your life that seems to once more need dramatic intervention and help. Let me suggest a simple expression common in recovery "let go and let God".

A friend once shared a principle that helped him to better grasp this simple expression of "let go and let God". He explained it was suggested to him to forget everything he thought he knew about recovery and to start completely new, completely fresh, as if he really did not know anything about recovery. All of his past actions and responses were to be forgotten, and he was to simply "let go and let God". That is what I suggest to you today to start fresh in your recovery and to simply yield to God. Ask God from the start about every recovery decision and even every decision of life, to ask God first or to "let go and let God".

The passage today from Philippians speaks to this very lesson when it instructs us to "Be anxious for nothing." That is the "let go" part, and it is not easy, but it is an important step and it is actually quite freeing. It simply means we are to trust God. The "let God" part is praying with thanksgiving and for our "requests to be made known to God". Not just some burdens but bring "everything by prayer" to the Lord. It is with this simple recovery and life principle that we can then have "the peace of God" in our hearts and minds. "Let go and let God" is a simple recovery lesson. I encourage you today to make the commitment to fully trust God so that you can indeed "let go and let God".

Prayer for today:

Dear Lord, I thank you that I can bring all my requests before you. Help me to truly follow the principle of "let go and let God" for I know I can trust you.

Notes of gratitude, progress, concerns, and prayers for today:

____

____

____

____

____

____

____

____

____

____

Day 81 of 100

Evidence of Hope

Jesus, once more deeply moved, came to the tomb. It was a cave with a stone laid across the entrance. [39] "Take away the stone," he said. "But, Lord," said Martha, the sister of the dead man, "by this time there is a bad odor, for he has been there four days." [40] Then Jesus said, "Did I not tell you that if you believe, you will see the glory of God?"
(John 11:38-40 NIV)

As you continue in your recovery journey and you attend meetings, counseling, church, recovery events, and do your readings, you may still feel uncertain about your recovery. You may still question if it is really possible for you. You may hear others share at meetings of being six months, or one year, or five years in recovery and yet you think to yourself, but that seems impossible for you. You cannot imagine how you will go that long without a drink or a drug and yet you continue on another day. You are still not convinced, but you continue on doing the next right thing nonetheless. As you continue on doing what you know you need to do to be successful in recovery at some point when you hear those same testimonies of individuals gratefully sharing that they are six months, or one year, or five years in recovery and yet this time you hear it differently. You hear those same testimonies, and now you hear hope. You have transitioned from a feeling of doubt to one of hope. What you hear them saying now is if they can do it, so can you. You accept their message of recovery as evidence of hope. As you hear these messages of clean and sober time, you now hear them as evidence of hope. You begin to see that with God in your life, it is possible, even for you.

The passage today from the Gospel of John is taken from the story of Lazarus and Jesus bringing him back to life. Lazarus had been dead for four days and his body was already in the tomb. There was no doubt he was dead and his family and friends had given up all hope, thinking for him it was too late. For many in recovery, it may seem your life was also destroyed. Many of your family and friends may feel it is too late for you and perhaps you also wonder if it is too late for you. But, with God in your life, all things are possible. Jesus told Martha, the sister of the dead man, “Did I not tell you that if you believe, you will see the glory of God?” What a great question! Consider this same promise for yourself today. If you believe in God, and if you have faith, you will see the glory of God in your life. With God in your life, there is absolutely reason for hope, because you can trust God and because you have seen evidence of hope. I encourage you to not limit God and to embrace the evidence of hope you see all around you. Bring God into your life, embrace hope, and be amazed at what God can do in your life.

Prayer for today:

Dear Lord, I am so grateful for the evidence of hope and that with you in my life I can be successful in recovery. Help me to continue to see the evidence of hope and to continue to put my hope and trust in you.

Notes of gratitude, progress, concerns, and prayers for today:

____

____

____

____

____

____

____

____

Day 82 of 100

Sick and Tired

Come to me, all you who are weary and burdened, and I will give you rest. [29] Take my yoke upon you and learn from me, for I am gentle and humble in heart, and you will find rest for your souls. (Matthew 11:28-29 NIV)

After years and decades in addiction, many addicts and alcoholics get to where they are simply "sick and tired of being sick and tired". The daily destructive routine of drinking from the first waking hours of the day until the last hour, that ends with passing out, often leads to being "sick and tired of being sick and tired." Combine that with being disconnected from family, friends, and co-workers and filling any interaction that happens with lies and half-truths to cover up what is really going on in your life. You are sick and tired physically, emotionally, and mentally. This is all matched with an apartment or house that also reflects a life in disarray, as you have no interest to clean-up, do the dishes, or make the bed. Everything about your life reflects the condition of being "sick and tired of being sick and tired". Perhaps this is how you have felt in the past, or perhaps this is how you feel right now. Sometimes this state of being sick and tired helps us acknowledge something needs to change. In fact something dramatic does need to change. Things cannot continue the way they are or the result will most certainly be tragic.

Are you "sick and tired of being sick and tired"? Coming to where you finally admit this to yourself is a great first step. However, do you go even further to make the personal commitment to make the dramatic changes in your life that are required? The passage today from Matthew includes the words of Jesus to people that may also be feeling sick and tried. Jesus implores them as he says, "Come to me". This is the first action step to take in response to being sick and tired. Come to Jesus. Put your faith and trust in God. This is very much like the Third Step of Recovery 'make a decision' to turn your life and will over to the care of God. Here Jesus pleads with the people who are “weary and burdened” to come to him and he “will give you rest.” I encourage you to take this dramatic step and to put your faith and trust in God. If you are truly “sick and tired of being sick and tired” then I encourage you to take this dramatic step to God. In recovery, it is absolutely true “if nothing changes, then nothing changes.” Start today to make the dramatic changes you need to make to be successful in recovery. Turn to God and he “will give you rest”. What a wonderful promise, a promise that Jesus himself makes to you today.

Prayer for today:

Dear Lord, Thank you that I do not need to continue being sick and tired. Thank you for the promise that you will give me rest for my weary condition and that with you in my life I can make the changes necessary to be successful in recovery.

Notes of gratitude, progress, concerns, and prayers for today:

____

____

____

____

____

____

____

____

____

____

Day 83 of 100

Restore Us to Sanity

When the disciples heard this, they were greatly astonished, saying, "Who then can be saved?" 26 But Jesus looked at them and said, "With man this is impossible, but with God all things are possible." (Matthew 19:25-26 ESV)

The recovery community is full of sayings, slogans, and quotes all intended to help individuals be successful in recovery. Each saying or quote is intended to highlight a principle of recovery. One such quote is "Insanity is doing the same thing over and over again and expecting a different result." It is a simple quote that is quite insightful and profound. Some individuals in recovery will have relapses followed by stays at rehab facilities, recovery houses, and starting over again with a familiar sequence. But, often the very same steps of recovery are performed just now with a renewed determination to be successful. However, another common quote of recovery is "If nothing changes, then nothing changes." This principle of doing recovery differently than before and making changes in this new attempt of recovery is absolutely critical. The concept of insanity and change is so foundational to recovery it is included in the Second Step of Recovery "We came to believe that a Power greater than ourselves could restore us to sanity."[49] This Second Step implies that the alcoholic and addict are not acting in a way that is sane as this step gives instruction to "restore us to sanity". Certainly, it does not mean that we are insane and beyond any hope, but it means we are acting in a way that is not sane, that makes little sense such as "doing the same thing over and over again and expecting a different result." To be successful in recovery, to be restored to sanity, means we need to change. We need to do recovery differently than before and this will ultimately require an internal change. It will require a spiritual change.

As you consider your recovery, you may feel perplexed, just as the disciples did in this passage from Matthew, and you may feel “greatly astonished” and wonder ‘who can recover’. Spiritual change is required and this spiritual change can come by bringing God into your life. It is with this spiritual change God can transform your life and bring about true change. Things that were impossible before are now possible with God. Consider that God says to you today “all things are possible”. God will do for you what you could not do for yourself. He will transform your life and give you the power to be successful in recovery and to live a brand new life. I encourage you to make this spiritual change and bring God into your life and allow him to restore you to sanity.

Prayer for today:

Dear Lord, thank you for restoring me to sanity. Help me to grow in this new life of spiritual change so that I can grow in my faith and also in my recovery.

Notes of gratitude, progress, concerns, and prayers for today:

____

____

____

____

____

____

____

____

____

Day 84 of 100

Another Great Day

And amazement seized them all, and they glorified God and were filled with awe, saying, "We have seen extraordinary things today."
(Luke 5:26 ESV)

There is a common expression in recovery of "One day at a time". This is a foundational principle of recovery. Yet, it is sometimes overlooked as not really significant. However, each and every day that you are clean and sober is indeed another great day! For the alcoholic and addict to go to bed at night with another day in recovery is another great day. Regardless of what else happened today, if you did not drink or use it is another great day. Whatever else might happen, you are able to handle these events of everyday life with a clear mind and you can have confidence God will help you through any situation or struggle of life. When you lay your head down at night, you can have peace and calm in your mind, body, and spirit and you can know it was another great day.

This passage today from Luke describes Jesus performing a miracle of healing a paralyzed man who was brought to Jesus by his friends. His friends took extreme measures to get their friend to Jesus by lowering him on a mat through the roof of the home. This man and his friends knew who to turn to for help and Jesus met his need in a mighty way, with a miracle. As you look to Jesus, he will meet your need as well and as you put your faith and trust in God, you will experience a miracle each and every day, a miracle of another day clean and sober. The people that witnessed the healing of this paralyzed man were amazed and gave thanks and praise to God, because they knew it was God's healing power that restored this man. For you today, it is a blessing of God's transforming power in your life that you can end another day clean and sober. As you continue to trust God, he will also guide you in all matters of life. As you reflect on this day, you can indeed know you "have seen extraordinary things today". I encourage you to recognize and be grateful for each and every day you are clean and sober. Give thanks and praise to God for the peace and calmness you have each evening as you lay your head down at night and as your celebrate another great day.

Prayer for today:

Dear Lord, help me to be mindful that each and every day in recovery is another great day and a day of "extraordinary things". I thank you for the miracle in my life of another day and of your grace and healing in my life.

Notes of gratitude, progress, concerns, and prayers for today:

____

____

____

____

____

____

____

____

____

____

Day 85 of 100

Your Greatest Need Is Spiritual

But seek first his kingdom and his righteousness, and all these things will be given to you as well. (Matthew 6:33 NIV)

As you continue to make progress in your recovery, you may see all the damage around you because of your addiction. You may see a long list of issues that you feel need to be addressed and resolved before you can truly make progress in recovery. You may have a mountain of bills, debts, and fines that need to be paid. You may have a suspended driver's license, you are eager to get reactivated. You may see many broken relationships you want to see restored. You may want a new job to afford your own apartment. These concerns may well be valid and appropriate to be addressed at some point. But it is important for all of us to understand, regardless of whatever our needs might be; our greatest need is always spiritual. We need to keep our relationship with God as our greatest need. As we continue to focus on God, this will help us stay focused on our recovery and will also help us properly prioritize the other mounting concerns.

The passage today from Matthew speaks to this key principle that our greatest need is always spiritual. It is easy to get side-tracked and change our focus on our needs and burdens of life. But this passage instructs us to "seek first his kingdom and his righteousness". It instructs us to remember our greatest need is spiritual; our greatest need is our relationship with God. Even more, this passage teaches that as we seek God first, "all these things will be given" to us as well. We need to stay focused on God. Certainly, it is important to seek wise counsel regarding any concerns we face. We will always have concerns of life, but it is important to stay focused on God and his will in our life. God wants us to address these valid concerns of life, but his schedule and priority may well differ from what we think is right. We need to yield to God and his will. Be patient and trust God, even in the everyday concerns of life. I encourage you today to be mindful that your greatest need is your relationship with God; your greatest need is always spiritual. Consider today the changes you need to make to reflect that your greatest need is spiritual.

Prayer for today:

Dear Lord, help me to stay focused on you and your will in my life and not to be overwhelmed with the issues of everyday life. Even today help me to be mindful that my greatest need is always spiritual.

Notes of gratitude, progress, concerns, and prayers for today:

____

____

____

____

____

____

____

____

____

____

Day 86 of 100

There Is a God

In the beginning God created the heavens and the earth. (Genesis 1:1 NIV)

There is a chapter in *Alcoholics Anonymous* called "We Agnostics" which speaks to individuals who may consider themselves either agnostics or atheists. Many individuals identify as agnostics or atheists and if you fall into this category, please know that I encourage you to consider the advice of *Alcoholics Anonymous* that asks you to "merely remain open-minded to the possibility that there was a Power greater"[50] than yourself. As you seek to be successful in recovery, be open to truly finding a power greater than yourself to help do for you what you could not do for yourself. *Alcoholics Anonymous* is a spiritual book with a spiritual solution to those struggling with alcohol or drug addiction. The spiritual solution truly begins when you acknowledge the possibility that there is a God. To this perspective, *Alcoholics Anonymous* describes a common experience in recovery:

> "Our human resources, as marshalled by the will, were not sufficient; they failed utterly. Lack of power, that was our dilemma. We had to find a power by which we could live, and it had to be a Power greater than ourselves. Obviously....we had to fearlessly face the proposition that either God is everything or else He is nothing. God either is, or He isn't. What was our choice to be?"[51]

It is likely that everyone, at some point in their life, questions the existence of God. This is one of the "big questions of life" and I think we all wrestle with this question at times. It is with this very perspective in mind I believe it is so amazing God wrote Genesis 1:1. It is as if God understood this would be one of the big questions of life for us humans and he was addressing this very question in the very first verse of the Bible. It was as if God could not wait to answer this fundamental question. As we all consider this question about the existence of God, he put this very first verse in the Bible that states "In the beginning God created the heavens and the earth." Or perhaps just the words "In the beginning God" would be enough for us to know that 'yes' there is a God. Consider for yourself there is a God in heaven and he is the ultimate "Higher Power". Whatever your beliefs are about God, I encourage you to continue to seek to find God and as you diligently seek him, he will reveal himself to you. The God of the Bible is a loving, caring, and compassionate God who is able to help you be successful in recovery. The God who created everything that exists is the same God who can help you be successful in recovery.

Prayer for today:

Dear Lord, I thank you for the book of Genesis and that you tell us in the very first verse that you were there in the beginning and that you created everything. Help me to trust you as the ultimate "Higher Power".

Notes of gratitude, progress, concerns, and prayers for today:

____

____

____

____

____

____

____

____

Let Go of Resentments

"You have heard that it was said, 'You shall love your neighbor and hate your enemy.' [44] But I say to you, Love your enemies and pray for those who persecute you, [45] so that you may be sons of your Father who is in heaven." (Matthew 5:43-45 ESV)

We have all experienced resentments at various points throughout our lives. It is a common and powerful human emotion. But, for the addict or alcoholic, holding on to resentments can have terrible outcomes. Resentments that are not properly dealt with often lead to frustration, anger, and relapse. There are countless types of resentments, but it seems they are most often directed at people, either individually or to some group of people. Perhaps you are reminded of some resentment you held in the past or even still have today. Resentments are many and varied: perhaps you did not get the help you needed, or you did not get the credit you deserved, or your therapist gave the wrong treatment, or your family did not trust you quickly enough, or the court made a terribly unfair decision, and many more. *Alcoholics Anonymous* describes resentment as "the 'number one' offender" at destroying recovery. Holding on to resentments can have tragic results, as the *Alcoholics Anonymous* describes below:

> "Resentment is the "number one'' offender. It destroys more alcoholics than anything else. From it stem all forms of spiritual disease, for we have been not only mentally and physically ill, we have been spiritually sick. When the spiritual malady is overcome, we straighten out mentally and physically."[52]

In the passage today from Matthew, Jesus describes a new command. A new command of how we are to treat our enemies. This new teaching has much to teach us in how to deal with resentments.

Jesus instructs us to embrace a new command to "Love your enemies and pray for those who persecute you." Jesus does not detail any criteria for this new approach only that we are to love and pray for them. Our first response may be "but what about if they..." and we can each fill in the blank with our own exception. However, the passage is quite clear, we are to love and pray for our enemies. Some in our recovery group have suggested praying each morning for those that we have current resentments. Pray each morning for 30 days. Pray for them in positive ways, pray for their good. This is a way of letting go of resentments towards people and moving instead to love and pray for them. I encourage you to consider today who you have resentments towards and I challenge you to pray for them for 30 days. During this time you will see a transformation. It may not change the other person, but it will change you.

Prayer for today:

Dear Lord, help me to let go of resentments. Help me to pray for 30 days for one individual that I still hold resentments towards. I will pray for the good of this person and for transformation of my heart and spirit as well.

Notes of gratitude, progress, concerns, and prayers for today:

____

____

____

____

____

____

Day 88 of 100

A Wonderful Thing

May the God of hope fill you with all joy and peace in believing, so that by the power of the Holy Spirit you may abound in hope.
(Romans 15:13 ESV)

Hope is an amazing human emotion. Hope is belief things will be better tomorrow and this belief can have many positive benefits. But, it is one thing to simply hope for a better tomorrow, for a better job, for a better apartment, for an arrest record to be cleared, or for one year in recovery. But, when we put our hope in God, the impact can transform our life. The key is where we put our hope and trust. When we put our hope and trust in God that can make all the difference. While this is absolutely true, we often take this to mean God will change all of our life circumstances. We may feel this means God will remove all of our "bad" situations and that is how he will transform our life. But as we seek God's will in all aspects of our life, he will give us peace and even joy. As we bring God into our life and seek his will, we will have joy and peace even in the midst of the storms of life. Truly putting our hope in God will enable us to have joy and peace in the midst of the storms. This type of life transformation is reflected in this quote from *Alcoholics Anonymous*:

> "And then probably the most wonderful thing that I have learned from the program—I've seen this in the A.A. Grapevine a lot of times, and I've had people say it to me personally, and I've heard people get up in meetings and say it—is this statement: "I came into A.A. solely for the purpose of sobriety, but it has been through A.A. that I have found God." I feel that is about the most wonderful thing that a person can do."[53]

Finding God is wonderful indeed. It is only by bringing God into our life that we can know true peace. Our problems may not all disappear, but as we put our hope and trust in God, we will have joy and peace in our life even as we go through struggles. I encourage you today to consider where you put your hope and trust. As you seek to honor God in all aspects of your life, even during many challenging and difficult times, he will enable you to have joy and peace. It is with this hope and trust in God you will be able to stay clean and sober. Even more than that, you will be able to stay clean and sober and have joy and peace as well.

Prayer for today:

Dear Lord, thank you for this wonderful truth that with you in my life I can have true joy and peace. Help me to be mindful that life will not be perfect, but I can always put my hope and trust in you.

Notes of gratitude, progress, concerns, and prayers for today:

____

____

____

____

____

____

____

____

____

____

Choose God

And if it is evil in your eyes to serve the Lord, choose this day whom you will serve....But as for me and my house, we will serve the Lord.
(Joshua 24:14-15 ESV)

Life is full of decisions, full of choices. Living in addiction, these decisions and choices were all geared towards getting the next drink or the next drug or perhaps simply trying to hide what we were really doing and how we were really living. There is a quote from the book *The Life You've Always Wanted* by John Ortberg that speaks to this topic of choice. He states:

> "Human behavior is a complex thing. But confession means saying that somewhere in the mix was a choice, and the choice was made by us, and it does not need to be excused, explained, or even understood. The choice needs to be forgiven. The slate has to be wiped clean."[54]

Human behavior is indeed a complicated thing, and Ortberg is correct that basically it comes down to our choices and decisions. Human behavior is full of the choices we all make every day. For those of us in addiction our past is full of bad choices and while we cannot undo those past choices, there are three things we can do now in response to those past choices. First, we can ask God for his forgiveness and fortunately, we can have confidence that he will forgive us from all of our past sins. Second, we can make the intentional choice today to bring God into our life. And third, from this point on starting today, we can wholeheartedly choose to honor God with our life and actions. We can choose God.

The passage today from Joshua 24 describes how Joshua had presented the people with a choice to either serve their "other" gods of the past or to serve the Lord God of heaven. Individuals living in addiction are, in essence, serving other gods as they are serving the god of alcohol or drugs. The instruction and question of Joshua is still valid for us today, "choose this day whom you will serve". Consider this question for yourself. How do you answer this question? If you respond to "choose God" I encourage you to ask God for forgiveness, to make the choice to bring God into your life, and then start today to choose to honor God with your life and actions. If your response is to "choose God" make a note on this page with today's date as a reminder of your decision to "choose God" and to live for God and to honor him with your life.

Prayer for today:

Dear Lord, forgive me of all my past sins. I am so unworthy, but I am so grateful for your grace, mercy, and forgiveness. Today I do "choose God". Please come into my life and help me live for you and to honor you with my brand new life with God.

Notes of gratitude, progress, concerns, and prayers for today:

____

____

____

____

____

____

____

____

____

Finding God

They know the truth about God because he has made it obvious to them. [20] For ever since the world was created, people have seen the earth and sky. Through everything God made, they can clearly see his invisible qualities—his eternal power and divine nature. So they have no excuse for not knowing God.
(Romans 1:19-20 NLT)

The books of *Alcoholics Anonymous* and *Narcotics Anonymous* both speak of a spiritual experience with God, where God is often referred to as a "Higher Power". These two leading recovery fellowships both encourage us to seek to find God and to have a spiritual experience. *Narcotics Anonymous* states, "The Narcotics Anonymous Program is spiritual. We strongly suggest that members make an attempt to find a Higher Power."[55] *Alcoholics Anonymous* goes even further stating:

> "The great fact is just this, and nothing less: That we have had deep and effective spiritual experiences* which have revolutionized our whole attitude toward life, toward our fellows and toward God's universe."[56]

But, many have not had a spiritual experience or do not have any faith and they are not sure how to find God or how to start the process of finding God?

The passage today from Romans is a great place to start for those that may be uncertain about God and uncertain how to start the process of finding God. Basically, the apostle Paul says that the created world itself is evidence of God and that the created world is evidence of a divine "Higher Power". This evidence, presented in the created world, is "obvious to them....Through everything God made, they can clearly see his invisibles qualities—his eternal power and divine nature." This great passage points out that we can start by looking at the created world around us as it all points to God, to a divine "Higher Power". The truth of this passage also reflects that the Bible was divinely inspired and written by God. This passage suggests we look at the created world around us in a fresh new way. As you look at the world from a new perspective, of seeking to find God, you will be able to "clearly see his invisible qualities" and "his "eternal power and divine nature". Yes, the created world itself points to God, and the Bible reveals even more about God as well. As you read, you will find out more about God and his great love for you and for the world. If you honestly seek to find God, he will reveal himself to you. I encourage you today to seek to find God and to have your own "spiritual experience" by bringing God into your life.

Prayer for today:

Dear Lord, I thank you for revealing yourself in the created world all around us and thank you for the Bible that reveals even more about your great love for the world and even for me.

Notes of gratitude, progress, concerns, and prayers for today:

____

____

____

____

____

____

____

____

Get to Know God

All Scripture is inspired by God and is useful to teach us what is true and to make us realize what is wrong in our lives. It corrects us when we are wrong and teaches us to do what is right.
(2 Timothy 3:16 NLT)

The books of *Alcoholics Anonymous* and *Narcotics Anonymous* instruct us to find God and to have a spiritual experience. Certainly, bringing God into your life and having a spiritual experience is critical for success in recovery and even success in life. But, after you find God and after you bring God into your life, then what? How do you continue to grow in your spiritual experience, in your relationship with God, in your faith, and in turn, grow in your recovery? There are many resources and many ways for learning more about God and growing in your faith. These various ways include reading books, praying, meditating and reflecting on God, singing songs of praise, performing service for others, going to church, attending Bible studies and many more. All these do help in nurturing your faith and increasing your knowledge of God. As you continue growing in your recovery, it is equally important to continue growing in your faith. Continue going to meetings, continue going to church, and do everything you should do for your recovery and do everything you should do to also grow in your faith.

But, perhaps the best way to get to know God is simply through reading his Word the Bible. The Bible is the primary way God reveals himself to us. Often we get distracted by all the other, perhaps more exciting, ways to read about spiritual matters and we forget or overlook the single best way to learn about God which is reading his Word. The passage today from 2 Timothy reminds us that the Bible is "inspired by God and is useful to teach us what is true." The Bible is written by God and is the primary way for us to learn about God and how to live a life that honors God. The issues of life that people faced 2000 years ago are still the same issues that we face today, only now with modern devices and settings, but the matters of the heart are still the same. As you read the Bible, perhaps one book at a time, you will see that the struggles people faced then are very similar to the issues that we face today. People still lie, cheat, steal, kill, abuse alcohol, abuse sex, desire what they don't have, lust, seek even more money and power, and the list goes on and on. God's Word addresses all these human failings and shows us how to live a life that honors God. I suggest you start by reading one book of the Bible, perhaps the Gospel of John, and as you read, look for one key insight in each reading that reveals something new about God and highlight it or underline it. I encourage you to remember the Bible is the primary way for us to learn about God and to grow in our relationship with God. Reading the Bible will help you get to know God and will help you in your recovery as well.

Prayer for today:

Dear Lord, thank you for your Word the Bible as the primary way for me to know you better. Help me to regularly read your Word and to grow in my knowledge and love for you.

Notes of gratitude, progress, concerns, and prayers for today:

____

____

____

____

____

____

Day 92 of 100

Go to Church

Let us think of ways to motivate one another to acts of love and good works. [25] And let us not neglect our meeting together, as some people do, but encourage one another. (Hebrews 10:24-25 NLT)

Many people in recovery understand the importance of meetings, such that there are several common sayings in the recovery community related to meetings. One such saying is "Seven days without a meeting makes one weak" and another is "Many meetings, many chances; few meetings, few chances; no meetings, no chances". Both of these sayings highlight the importance of attending meetings. Many individuals in recovery will share the importance meetings have played in their recovery. *Alcoholics Anonymous* and *Narcotics Anonymous* both stress the importance of attending meetings regularly. *Narcotics Anonymous* describes how many feel about meetings when they first start attending:

> "In time, we can relax and enjoy the atmosphere of recovery. Meetings strengthen our recovery. We may be scared at first because we don't know anyone. Some of us think that we don't need meetings. However, when we hurt, we go to a meeting and find relief."[57]

This description above could also describe attending church. Does that description match feelings you have had in the past towards attending church? The AA and NA fellowships also stress the importance of having a spiritual experience by having a personal relationship with God. There is another book that is recognized by many as the authority about having a spiritual experience with God and that book is the Bible. It is interesting that, just like the books of *Alcoholics Anonymous* and *Narcotics Anonymous*, the Bible also gives guidance on attending church and other places of worship. The passage today from Hebrews encourages us to "not neglect our meeting together". In addition attending worship and fellowship on a weekly basis is also included in the Ten Commandments as "Remember the Sabbath day, to keep it holy." (Exodus 20:8 ESV) Just as you carefully consider the meetings you attend also carefully consider the church you attend. There will not be a perfect church, but I encourage you to find a church where you can grow in your knowledge of the Bible, in your relationship with God, and also with other believers. However, do not delay. Start this very week and do not wait until you find a church "you like." Go to church. Go to church somewhere this Sunday even if you have not yet found the church you want to call your home church. Attending meetings are important for your recovery and attending church is important for the spiritual part of your recovery. Start this week and go to church.

Prayer for today:

Dear Lord, thank you for the blessing of recovery meetings and thank you for the blessing of church "meetings" as well. Help me to start this week and go to church somewhere this week.

Notes of gratitude, progress, concerns, and prayers for today:

____

____

____

____

____

____

____

Day 93 of 100

Know God's Will

And going a little farther he fell on his face and prayed, saying, "My Father, if it be possible, let this cup pass from me; nevertheless, not as I will, but as you will." (Matthew 26:39 ESV)

Seeking God's will is of vital concern to the fellowships of AA and NA. God's will is so critical it is included in the Twelve Steps in Step Three in *Narcotics Anonymous* as "*We made a decision to turn our will and our lives over to the care of God* as we understood Him*"*[58] Part of this is to take our self-centered focus off of ourselves, but another reason is to put our focus squarely onto God as we grow more in our spiritual life and in our relationship with God. Seeking God's will in our life gives us a higher purpose, a higher calling. Our purpose of life will change from having worldly goals, material goals, or perhaps even no goals at all to spiritual goals. These newfound spiritual goals include having a genuine concern to help others in recovery, a desire to love and care for people, and even a heartfelt desire to honor God in all we do. This is quite a transformation indeed. *Narcotics Anonymous* describes this as:

> "I was told that perhaps I should seek God's will first, and then conform my will to His. Today, I pray only for His will for me and the power to carry it out on a daily basis, and all is well. I have found that His gifts are without number when I consistently turn my will and my life over to His care."[59]

The passage today in Matthew also reflects the importance the Bible places on God's will. In this passage, the Lord Jesus is praying the night before He was to go to the cross. Jesus is full of emotion as it states "he fell on his face and prayed". Jesus, being fully human and fully God, prays "if it be possible, let this cup pass from me". It is a genuine prayer as Jesus presents his requests to the father. However, Jesus does not stop there. He adds "not as I will, but as you will." What a great example for us to follow! Regardless of what our circumstances of life might be, the example here is we are certainly to pray for our requests, but not to stop there. We are to pray for God's will in our life, whatever that might be. Let me suggest these four steps as a guide for knowing God's will in our life:

1) Read the Bible seeking guidance from God's Word.
2) Seek wise counsel from trusted godly individuals.
3) Bring your request before God and pray for his will.
4) Trust God and respond as he is directing you.

I encourage you to bring all your requests before God, seek God's will in your life, and trust he will direct your paths, then be obedient and responds as God leads you. You will be amazed at what God can do in your life.

Prayer for today:

Dear Lord, help me to prayerfully seek your will in my life and help me to have the obedience and courage to respond as you direct.

Notes of gratitude, progress, concerns, and prayers for today:

____

____

____

____

____

____

____

This Great Truth

Do you not know? Have you not heard? The Lord is the everlasting God, the Creator of the ends of the earth. He will not grow tired or weary, and his understanding no one can fathom. [29] He gives strength to the weary and increases the power of the weak. (Isaiah 40:28-29 NIV)

The concept of a power greater than ourselves is foundational to both *Alcoholics Anonymous* and *Narcotics Anonymous* and indeed to success in recovery. Many in recovery had tried many times to be successful in recovery, only to fail again and again. We felt desperate, hopeless, and at times we felt as though it might not be possible for us. Many have tried different routines, habits, locations, and strategies for recovery, but nothing worked. *Alcoholics Anonymous* describes this scenario accurately when it states:

> "If a mere code of morals or a better philosophy of life were sufficient to overcome alcoholism, many of us would have recovered long ago. But we found that such codes and philosophies did not save us, no matter how much we tried.... Lack of power, that was our dilemma. We had to find a power by which we could live, and it had to be a *Power greater than ourselves.* Obviously."[60]

The issue is not a lack of willpower or determination the issue is a lack of power. You may have confirmed this with genuine attempts at recovery on your own power, only to relapse again. The Twelve Steps of Recovery affirm this point with Step Two "*We came to believe that a Power greater than ourselves could restore us to sanity.*"[61] Yes, we needed a power greater than ourselves indeed. Once you understand and accept this basic truth, you are making progress in recovery. Once you accept this truth, that success in recovery requires a power greater than yourself that is a huge step.

This step will then prepare you for the next step which is to understand where this newfound power will come from. The passage today from Isaiah describes this great truth of the "power greater than ourselves" as "The Lord is the everlasting God". This passage presents this great truth to us as the first time we might be hearing it. "Do you not know? Have you not heard?" For many it is the first time the God of the Bible is considered as this "power greater than ourselves". This passage confidently proclaims this great truth. If God is truly the "the everlasting God...Creator of the ends of the earth" then he is certainly more than able to help us be successful in recovery. I encourage you to consider today this passage is indeed true and God is able to give "strength to the weary" and to increase "power to the weak". Accept this great truth for yourself today and bring God into your life.

Prayer for today:

Dear Lord, thank you for this great truth and this great hope for the weary. Help me to embrace this newfound power in you as I desperately need a power great than myself.

Notes of gratitude, progress, concerns, and prayers for today:

____

____

____

____

____

____

____

The One Year Rule

You shall love the Lord your God with all your heart and with all your soul and with all your might. [6] And these words that I command you today shall be on your heart.
(Deuteronomy 6:5-6 ESV)

Many in recovery will be familiar with the recovery “rule” to not start any new dating relationship until you have at least one year in recovery. This is wise guidance for sure; but it is not a rule of *Alcoholics Anonymous* or *Narcotics Anonymous*. It is a well-known principle, but it is not really mentioned in either of these books. Relationships are absolutely important and that is part of how God designed us, as relational beings, but for those during their first year of recovery, it is critical to stay focused on recovery. There is so much in early recovery that is still in need of healing and simply getting emotionally and physically healthy again that it is wise to not start any new relationships until after one year of recovery. Likely, you will be feeling emotions that you have not felt for quite some time. You not only need to be clean and sober, but you need to heal as well. *Narcotics Anonymous* speaks about relationships and it mentions what is the most important relationship for those in recovery to work on:

> “Since this time I have worked on the most important relationship in my life: the one with my higher power, God.”[62]

A key principle of this devotional is to be committed to do whatever is necessary to be successful in recovery, because unless you are clean and sober, nothing else will matter. Being successful in recovery and getting a one year foundation of recovery is important and should not be quickly dismissed. As our passage today indicates, there is a relationship to nurture and that is your relationship with God. “You shall love the Lord your God with all your heart.” Before you can truly love someone else, you need to have a restored relationship with God. As you continue on in your first year of recovery, you may face the opportunity to start a new relationship and I encourage you to remember the commitment you made to do whatever is necessary to be successful in recovery. Prayerfully seek God's direction before starting any new relationship. As with any important decision, seek godly counsel. Be cautious and wise to not jeopardize your recovery. The one year rule is another way to trust God and to seek his will in your life. I encourage you to trust God to bring just the right person into your life at just the right time.

Prayer for today:

Dear Lord, I love you and I am so grateful for your great love and compassion saving me from the pit of addiction. Give me wisdom and guidance before I start any new relationship. Help me to trust you and to yield to your will in my life even regarding any new relationship.

Notes of gratitude, progress, concerns, and prayers for today:

____

____

____

____

____

____

____

____

Day 96 of 100

Do Not Limit God

I said, 'You are my servant'; I have chosen you and have not rejected you.[10] So do not fear, for I am with you; do not be dismayed, for I am your God. I will strengthen you and help you; I will uphold you with my righteous right hand. (Isaiah 41:9-10 NIV)

Nothing is impossible for God. No one is so far in the depths of addiction they are beyond the reach of God. You may feel you are beyond hope, that the life you lived was too evil and terrible, you are beyond God. To that I say 'do not limit God'. Regardless of where you came from in your addiction, God can rescue you. God can restore you and God absolutely wants to forgive you. As you continue in recovery, it is important to be mindful of the principle to do whatever is necessary to be successful in recovery. And while that is true, it is also important to be open to what else God has for you. God has rescued you from your addiction for a reason, for a purpose. What else does God have for you and for your future? With your life experience, you are uniquely qualified to help others as only someone with your specific addiction battle and life story can. You can help others to also be successful in recovery. The quote below from the *Narcotics Anonymous* gives us a glimpse of how God can change the direction of our lives to be better able to help others:

> "Early in recovery, through prodding from many of the "older" members of the fellowship, I earned a GED.... (and later) In spite of these challenges, I graduated with a master's degree in social work. In one lifetime God has allowed me two chances to live, and I am in a position to help others avoid some of the painful experiences I suffered through. To me, this is the greatest gift I have received."[63]

If you woke up today and you are still breathing, then God is not done with you yet! This quote above describes how God used this middle-age man to get his GED and then go on to college and then to earn a master's degree in social work. This was all done so he could be better prepared to help others. Consider for yourself what God might have for you in your future, especially when you 'do not limit God'. In the passage today from Isaiah, God says he has "not rejected you" and he will "strengthen you and help you" and he will uphold you with his "righteous right hand". God is for you! God has a purpose and plan for your life. Be open to what God has for you and be mindful that God saved you for a reason. Regardless of what your circumstances are right now, 'do not limit God' and consider God has a purpose and a plan for your future.

Prayer for today:

Dear Lord, I thank you that you have chosen me and that you are my God. Help me to not limit what you can do in my life and help me to be open to your purpose and plan for my life whatever that might be. .

Notes of gratitude, progress, concerns, and prayers for today:

____

____

____

____

____

____

____

____

Day 97 of 100

You Can Have Joy

These things I have spoken to you, that my joy may be in you, and that your joy may be full.[12] "This is my commandment, that you love one another as I have loved you."
(John 15:11-12 ESV)

In the depths of your addiction, it may seem that a life of recovery is just not possible. It may seem that even if you decide to seek help that recovery is just not possible for you and certainly not a life that would have peace and joy. Perhaps that is how you feel right now. You may feel that 30 or 60 days is possible maybe, but a lifetime of recovery just does not seem possible. Yet you know that a life in addiction will only end in tragedy. However, many thousands and even millions of people have felt exactly the same way you feel right now and yet they went on to change the direction of their lives to be successful in recovery through the strength and power of God, the one true Higher Power. Regardless of how hopeless you may feel right now, recovery is possible; even a life full of peace and joy. *Alcoholics Anonymous* and *Narcotics Anonymous* both speak of a spiritual change by making a decision to surrender your life and will to the care of God. Life can begin to change when you put God first and seek every day to do the next right thing. It sounds simple, but it is certainly not easy. This quote below from the *Narcotics Anonymous* gives us insight how your life can change when you bring God into your life.

> "God helps us as we help each other. Life takes on a new meaning, a new joy, and a quality of being and feeling worthwhile. We become spiritually refreshed and are glad to be alive. One aspect of our spiritual awakening comes through the new understanding of our Higher Power that we develop by sharing another addict's recovery. Yes, we are a vision of hope."[64]

In the passage today from John, Jesus speaks to the disciples about joy. But it is not a joy that magically shows up one day. Rather, it is a joy that comes as we bring God into our life and we are open to being "spiritually refreshed". Jesus gives the disciples a simple instruction of how to have this joy and the command is to "love one another as I have loved you". This is much like the message of *Narcotics Anonymous* above that "God helps us as we help each other". Jesus teaches the disciples their "joy may be full" as they "love one another" and that is the same message for us today. As you grow close to God and in your "spiritual awakening" you will also grow in joy and your life will take "on a new meaning". With God, your life can be different. You can not only be clean and sober, but you can have joy as well. I encourage you to bring God into your life and seek to honor God as you love and care for others.

Prayer for today:

Dear Lord, thank you for the spiritual awakening and the joy I have found in you. Help me to love and care for others as an expression of my love for you.

Notes of gratitude, progress, concerns, and prayers for today:

____

____

____

____

____

____

Day 98 of 100

Unmerited Grace

When people work, their wages are not a gift, but something they have earned. [5]But people are counted as righteous, not because of their work, but because of their faith in God who forgives sinners.
(Romans 4:4-5 NLT)

We are taught at an early age we only get what we have earned. When we work at a job for 40 hours a week, our employer is obligated to pay us for those 40 hours. It is not a gift, it is something we have earned by working those hours. This is a common understanding and seems to be fair and to make sense as well. When we work for our employer, we get paid. However, becoming a Christian is different. We do not earn our salvation. We do not perform a certain number of "good deeds" to earn a right standing with God. Our right standing with God is a free gift of God. The Third Step of Recovery indicates this same type of free gift. It suggests that we can have a very different outcome simply by putting our faith and trust in God. *Narcotics Anonymous* describes it as:

> "*We made a decision to turn our will and our lives over to the care of God* as we understood Him.... The word decision implies action. This decision is based on faith. We have only to believe that the miracle that we see working in the lives of clean addicts can happen to any addict with the desire to change."[65]

The Third Step of Recovery is really about faith. It is about putting our faith and trust in God and believing in a miracle. When we take the Third Step of Recovery, we are not completing a long list of tasks or projects or activities such that we have then earned any grace. Rather, we are simply making a decision. We are taking a step of faith towards God. This *Narcotics Anonymous* quote is like the passage for today from Romans in that God's grace and mercy to us is not earned. God extends his grace and mercy to us even though it is not earned. It is unmerited grace! The passage wonderfully expresses this great truth "because of their faith in God who forgives sinners". We are all sinners! We are all graciously granted unmerited grace and forgiveness from God, simply because of our decision to put our faith and trust in God. I encourage you to make this decision today to put your faith and trust in God and to accept God's unmerited grace. It is by this miracle of faith that you can begin a brand new life; a life where you are successful in recovery and a life where you leave the past in the past and accept God's free gift of "unmerited grace."

Prayer for today:

Dear Lord, thank you for your free gift of "unmerited grace". I am forever grateful that I am saved by grace through faith in the Lord Jesus Christ. Help me to share this wonderful message to others.

Notes of gratitude, progress, concerns, and prayers for today:

____

____

____

____

____

____

____

____

____

Day 99 of 100

Be Fully Prepared

So Philip ran to him and heard him reading Isaiah the prophet and asked, "Do you understand what you are reading?" [31] And he said, "How can I, unless someone guides me?" And he invited Philip to come up and sit with him. (Acts 8:30-31 ESV)

Regardless of where you are at in your recovery, there will eventually be a "big day" when you are faced with taking the next big step forward in your recovery. This big day may be when you leave your rehab facility, or when you leave a half-way recovery house, or move out to your own apartment, or perhaps move back home to your family. All of these events and many more, all make up various big days in your recovery and in your life. It is important you take full advantage of all the resources available so you will be fully prepared and ready for when your big day arrives. There will be a time when it is your turn to say goodbye to everyone in your facility, apartment, or house and it is your turn to walk out the door to a brand new situation. It is critical you are indeed prepared. It is important for you to use all the resources available to you so you can be prepared and ready when your day arrives. Read all the books and material recommended, meet with your counselor and actually engage with them, attend all the meetings and be active, and faithfully take any prescribed medication as well. Do everything possible so you will be as prepared as possible for when your big day arrives and you are the one to walk out the door to your next big step forward in recovery. *Narcotics Anonymous* suggests the same as it recommends you actually read their book on recovery:

> "Many books have been written about the nature of addiction. This book concerns itself with the nature of recovery. If you are an addict and have found this book, please give yourself a break and read it."[66]

In our passage for today from Acts, the apostle Philip came upon a man reading from the book of Isaiah and he ran to him and began an interesting exchange. This brief dialog is a good model for us today. Philip asked him a great question, "Do you understand what you are reading?" Perhaps that is a good question for you today as you are reading and trying to grow in your recovery and your faith. The response from the individual was also a great response for us to model "How can I, unless someone guides me?" And then he invited Philip to "come up and sit with him" and to give him instruction. Be open to instruction and be open to learning. Take full advantage of all the resources at your current stage of recovery so you can learn as much as possible and to be fully prepared for your next big day in recovery.

Prayer for today:

Dear Lord, help me to learn as much as possible now so that I can be fully prepared for my next step in recovery. Bring trusted individuals to teach me and direct me in your truth.

Notes of gratitude, progress, concerns, and prayers for today:

____

____

____

____

____

____

____

Day 100 of 100

Continue to Trust God No Matter What

Trust in the Lord with all your heart; do not depend on your own understanding.[6] Seek his will in all you do, and he will show you which path to take. (Proverbs 3:5-6 NLT)

The message for today is simply to continue to trust God, no matter what happens. Regardless of our situation, we are to put our "trust in the Lord" and to not depend on our "own understanding." One thing we know for sure is life will continue to show up, bad things will still happen and good things will still happen. We might be doing everything right and yet bad things will happen. It is important to remember we are to simply trust God no matter what. Regardless of what might happen today or tomorrow, we are to continue to trust God for our recovery and even for everyday matters of life. Narc*otics Anonymous* reminds us of this truth:

> "We learned to trust God for help daily. Living just for today relieves the burden of the past and the fear of the future. We learned to take whatever actions are necessary and to leave the results in the hands of our Higher Power."[67]

The passage today from Proverbs has a simple and yet clear message; we are to trust God. In fact, we are instructed to "Trust in the Lord with all your heart". No matter what may happen, fair or not, good or bad, we are to trust God. Yield to God and trust him for help and guidance. We are to trust God and not depend on our "own understanding." The teachings of *Alcoholics Anonymous* and *Narcotics Anonymous* in the Third Step of Recovery reflect this message of Proverbs to "Seek his will in all you do." As you seek God's will in all aspects of life, he will give you guidance and wisdom to know just what to do and "he will show you which path to take." As you grow in your faith and in your recovery, I encourage you to renew your commitment to do whatever is necessary to be successful in recovery. As you trust God, no matter what happens, you can be successful in recovery and you can live a dramatically changed life. Continue to trust God no matter what happens and be amazed at what God can do in your life.

Prayer for today:

Dear Lord, thank you that I can trust you no matter what happens. Help me to trust you when bad times come and when good times come as well. Help me to always seek your will and to have the wisdom and courage to follow your paths.

Notes of gratitude, progress, concerns, and prayers for today:

____

____

____

____

____

____

____

____

____

____

Extra Day 1

A Spiritual Solution

And he said to him, "You shall love the Lord your God with all your heart and with all your soul and with all your mind. [38] This is the great and first commandment." (Matthew 22:37-38 ESV)

There are many paths that lead to addiction. Everyone has their own story of how they came to a life of addiction. There is no single road. The road to addiction is many and varied. But, at some level, every addict is seeking to fill a hole inside. Some refer to it as a God-sized hole that only God can fill. Unfortunately, we try to fill this hole, this void, with many other things hoping that this drug or drink or perhaps even a person or thing might fill the void. We unknowingly put something else in place of God; we have made something else an idol that we unfortunately came to worship. This hole is truly something that only God can fill and until we acknowledge that truth we will not be successful in recovery and we will not have inner peace. *Narcotics Anonymous* describes it as:

> "Based on our experience, we believe that every addict, including the potential addict, suffers from an incurable disease of body, mind, and spirit. We were in the grip of a hopeless dilemma, the solution of which is spiritual in nature. Therefore, this book will deal with spiritual matters."[68]

In some ways, it does not seem to make sense. How can my addiction require a spiritual solution? How can all these years of suffering in my addiction end up needing a spiritual solution, needing God? And yet as we look at the millions of people in AA and NA fellowships that have been successful in recovery, we see it works. The spiritual solution does indeed work. These two fellowships point to a common solution, a spiritual solution. The passage for today from Matthew is another way of describing the spiritual solution. In this passage, Jesus states "You shall love the Lord your God with all your heart and with all your soul and with all your mind." Put God first in your life, before everything else. That is how to fill the God-sized hole by putting God first! This verse really is speaking about Step Three of Recovery "We made a decision to turn our will and our lives over to the care of God as we understood Him."[69] We turn our life over to God, we love God above all else. I encourage you to turn your life over to God. Bring God into your life and love God with all your heart and you will fill the God-sized hole with the only one who can truly fill it and you will find the spiritual solution.

Prayer for today:

Dear Lord, thank you for filling my God-sized hole that only you could fill and thank you for not giving up on me. Help me to grow in my love for you and to share that great message with others so they can also be rescued.

Notes of gratitude, progress, concerns, and prayers for today:

____

____

____

____

____

____

____

____

____

____

Extra Day 2

How Will You Respond?

And when they had inflicted many blows upon them, they threw them into prison, ordering the jailer to keep them safely. [24]Having received this order, he put them into the inner prison and fastened their feet in the stocks. [25] About midnight Paul and Silas were praying and singing hymns to God. (Acts 16:23-25 ESV)

One thing we all know for sure is hard times will come; bad things will happen. Even if we are in recovery, or if we are now believers, or if we pray every day, or if we go to church every Sunday, bad things will still happen. It may be even when we do everything right, somehow bad things still happen. Life is not perfect, life is not fair, sometimes bad things happen. The real question is "how will we respond". When bad times come, you may be tempted to drink or use. It is also possible when good times come, you may be tempted to drink or use. It is important to be mindful of another common recovery saying, "Nothing is so bad a drink won't make it worse". Every day it is important how we respond to bad times and good times and we need to remember regardless of what happens, do not drink or use.

The passage today from Acts describes Paul and Silas being arrested, beaten and thrown into prison, and then being bound in an inner prison cell to make sure they did not escape. They were treated harshly and unjustly. This should not have happened to them. They should not have been treated so unfairly; and yet they were. They had every reason to be furious and upset with the civil officials, the prison guards, and perhaps even at God as well. But instead the passage says "About midnight Paul and Silas were praying and singing hymns to God." What an amazing passage! What an amazing lesson of response for us today! Paul and Silas were joyful despite their life circumstances. Despite what happened to them, they trusted God and honored God with their response. For us today, regardless of what happens to us, we need to stay focused on God and trust God. We need to trust God even when bad things happen and continue to honor God. When bad times come or good times come, the true question is "how will we respond". Regardless of your life circumstances, today or tomorrow, you are to respond in a way that honors God and supports your recovery. How will you respond to your current life circumstances or when bad times come in the future? I encourage you to be joyful, to trust God, and to honor God with your response. You can be confident that God will help you with either a miracle or with the wisdom and courage through the struggle. Whatever happens today respond in a way that honors God.

Prayer for today:

Dear Lord, help me to trust you despite my circumstances. Help me to understand that bad times and good times will still come and I need to focus on you and trust you and honor you with my response.

Notes of gratitude, progress, concerns, and prayers for today:

____

____

____

____

____

____

____

____

____

Extra Day 3

Remember There Is Always Hope with God

And so, Lord, where do I put my hope?
My only hope is in you.
(Psalm 39:7 NLT)

As you progress forward in your recovery, you may get past many of the early struggles and issues of early recovery only to face the everyday struggles and issues of life. Even with God in your life and being successful in recovery, bad things will still happen and you will still have various challenges of life that will often be quite difficult. However, remember you are not alone. God is still with you, just as close as when you first brought God into your life.

But, even now, I encourage you to remember that there is always hope with God even in the everyday struggles of life. The spiritual transformation that *Alcoholics Anonymous* talks about is a continuing spiritual transformation:

> "My physical being has certainly undergone a transformation, but the major transformation has been spiritual. The hopelessness has been replaced by abundant hope and sincere faith."[70]

The passage from Psalm 39 reminds us our hope is in God. Unfortunately, we do tend to drift away from God and the biblical truths of God, but we need to be mindful there is always hope with God. Psalm 39 presents a great question "where do I put my hope?" It was a great question then and even for us today. Where do you put your hope today? Do you put your hope in your own power, in a program, or perhaps in other people? King David, in this passage, declares "My only hope is in you." The God of the Bible is the one who is able to help you. The Lord God is able to meet your needs for recovery and even the everyday struggles of life. God is a great God and you can put your hope and trust in him. This passage and the *Alcoholics Anonymous* quote show a spiritual change by looking to God for help. As you bring God into your life and as you grow in your faith in God, you can have confidence that God will help you. You are not alone, God is with you and will help you every step along the way. Embrace this great truth that you can indeed put your hope and trust in God and he will help you. Hold fast to the truth there is always hope with God because he is the one who is able to help you. Continue to grow in your faith and continue to do the next right thing. As you bring God into your life and grow in your relationship with God you will be even more confident there is always hope with God.

Prayer for today:

Dear Lord, I thank you because you are the one who is able to help me. I know you are a great God, help me to understand my only hope is in you.

Notes of gratitude, progress, concerns, and prayers for today:

____

____

____

____

____

____

____

____

____

Footnotes

---

[1] Bill W., Alcoholics Anonymous: The Story of How Many Thousands of Men and Women Have Recovered from Alcoholism, (New York City NY, Alcoholics Anonymous World Services, Inc., 2001), 386-387.

[2] Bill W., Alcoholics Anonymous: The Story of How Many Thousands of Men and Women Have Recovered from Alcoholism, (New York City NY, Alcoholics Anonymous World Services, Inc., 2001), 475.

[3] Narcotics Anonymous, 6th ed. (Van Nuys, CA, Narcotics Anonymous World Services, Inc., 2008), 17.

[4] Bill W., Alcoholics Anonymous: The Story of How Many Thousands of Men and Women Have Recovered from Alcoholism, (New York City NY, Alcoholics Anonymous World Services, Inc., 2001), 84.

[5] Narcotics Anonymous, 6th ed. (Van Nuys, CA, Narcotics Anonymous World Services, Inc., 2008), 385.

[6] Bill W., Alcoholics Anonymous: The Story of How Many Thousands of Men and Women Have Recovered from Alcoholism, (New York City NY, Alcoholics Anonymous World Services, Inc., 2001), 24-25.

[7] Narcotics Anonymous, 6th ed. (Van Nuys, CA, Narcotics Anonymous World Services, Inc., 2008), 374.

[8] Bill W., Alcoholics Anonymous: The Story of How Many Thousands of Men and Women Have Recovered from Alcoholism, (New York City NY, Alcoholics Anonymous World Services, Inc., 2001), 55.

[9] Bill W., Alcoholics Anonymous: The Story of How Many Thousands of Men and Women Have Recovered from Alcoholism, (New York City NY, Alcoholics Anonymous World Services, Inc., 2001), 100.

[10] Bill W., Alcoholics Anonymous: The Story of How Many Thousands of Men and Women Have Recovered from Alcoholism,

(New York City NY, Alcoholics Anonymous World Services, Inc., 2001), 12.

[11] Bill W., Alcoholics Anonymous: The Story of How Many Thousands of Men and Women Have Recovered from Alcoholism, (New York City NY, Alcoholics Anonymous World Services, Inc., 2001), 187.

[12] Ibid., 192.

[13] Danny Simmons, My Moment of Truth in Rehab, 5/14/2015, Accessed: 9/30/2020, URL: https://www.guideposts.org/better-living/health-and-wellness/addiction-and-recovery/my-moment-of-truth-in-rehab

[14] Richard Dawkins, The God Delusion, (New York, NY, Houghton Mifflin Company, 2006), 31,158.

[15] Bill W., Alcoholics Anonymous: The Story of How Many Thousands of Men and Women Have Recovered from Alcoholism, (New York City NY, Alcoholics Anonymous World Services, Inc., 2001), 276.

[16] Bill W., Alcoholics Anonymous: The Story of How Many Thousands of Men and Women Have Recovered from Alcoholism, (New York City NY, Alcoholics Anonymous World Services, Inc., 2001), 337.

[17] Narcotics Anonymous, 6th ed. (Van Nuys, CA, Narcotics Anonymous World Services, Inc., 2008), 17.

[18] Narcotics Anonymous, 6th ed. (Van Nuys, CA, Narcotics Anonymous World Services, Inc., 2008), 149.

[19] Bill W., Alcoholics Anonymous: The Story of How Many Thousands of Men and Women Have Recovered from Alcoholism, (New York City NY, Alcoholics Anonymous World Services, Inc., 2001), 188.

[20] Bill W., Alcoholics Anonymous: The Story of How Many Thousands of Men and Women Have Recovered from Alcoholism, (New York City NY, Alcoholics Anonymous World Services, Inc., 2001), 25.

[21] Bill W., Alcoholics Anonymous: The Story of How Many Thousands of Men and Women Have Recovered from Alcoholism, (New York City NY, Alcoholics Anonymous World Services, Inc., 2001), 25.

[22] Narcotics Anonymous, 6th ed. (Van Nuys, CA, Narcotics Anonymous World Services, Inc., 2008), 17.

[23] Narcotics Anonymous, 6th ed. (Van Nuys, CA, Narcotics Anonymous World Services, Inc., 2008), 17.

[24] Narcotics Anonymous, 6th ed. (Van Nuys, CA, Narcotics Anonymous World Services, Inc., 2008), 17.

[25] Narcotics Anonymous, 6th ed. (Van Nuys, CA, Narcotics Anonymous World Services, Inc., 2008), 17.

[26] Narcotics Anonymous, 6th ed. (Van Nuys, CA, Narcotics Anonymous World Services, Inc., 2008), 17.

[27] Narcotics Anonymous, 6th ed. (Van Nuys, CA, Narcotics Anonymous World Services, Inc., 2008), 17.

[28] Spiritual Kindergarten: Christian Perspectives on the Twelve Steps, (Brea, CA, Christian Recovery international, 2008),48-49.

[29] Narcotics Anonymous, 6th ed. (Van Nuys, CA, Narcotics Anonymous World Services, Inc., 2008), 17.

[30] Narcotics Anonymous, 6th ed. (Van Nuys, CA, Narcotics Anonymous World Services, Inc., 2008), 17.

[31] Narcotics Anonymous, 6th ed. (Van Nuys, CA, Narcotics Anonymous World Services, Inc., 2008), 17.

[32] Narcotics Anonymous, 6th ed. (Van Nuys, CA, Narcotics Anonymous World Services, Inc., 2008), 41.

[33] Dale and Juanita Ryan, Spiritual Kindergarten: Christian Perspectives on the Twelve Steps, (Brea, CA, Christian Recovery International, 1999), 74.

[34] Narcotics Anonymous, 6th ed. (Van Nuys, CA, Narcotics Anonymous World Services, Inc., 2008), 17.

[35] Narcotics Anonymous, 6th ed. (Van Nuys, CA, Narcotics Anonymous World Services, Inc., 2008), 17.

[36] Narcotics Anonymous, 6th ed. (Van Nuys, CA, Narcotics Anonymous World Services, Inc., 2008), 17.

[37] Bill W., Alcoholics Anonymous: The Story of How Many Thousands of Men and Women Have Recovered from Alcoholism, (New York City NY, Alcoholics Anonymous World Services, Inc., 2001), 457.

[38] Bill W., Alcoholics Anonymous: The Story of How Many Thousands of Men and Women Have Recovered from Alcoholism, (New York City NY, Alcoholics Anonymous World Services, Inc., 2001), 70.

[39] Bill W., Alcoholics Anonymous: The Story of How Many Thousands of Men and Women Have Recovered from Alcoholism, (New York City NY, Alcoholics Anonymous World Services, Inc., 2001), 188.

[40] Bill W., Alcoholics Anonymous: The Story of How Many Thousands of Men and Women Have Recovered from Alcoholism, (New York City NY, Alcoholics Anonymous World Services, Inc., 2001), 324,326.

[41] Richmond W., Twenty-Four Hours a Day, (Daytona Beach, FL, Hazelden Publishing, 2013), Feb.21.

[42] Bill W., Alcoholics Anonymous: The Story of How Many Thousands of Men and Women Have Recovered from Alcoholism, (New York City NY, Alcoholics Anonymous World Services, Inc., 2001), 45.

[43] Bill W., Alcoholics Anonymous: The Story of How Many Thousands of Men and Women Have Recovered from Alcoholism, (New York City NY, Alcoholics Anonymous World Services, Inc., 2001), 316-317.

[44] Narcotics Anonymous, 6th ed. (Van Nuys, CA, Narcotics Anonymous World Services, Inc., 2008), 249.

[45] Bill W., Alcoholics Anonymous: The Story of How Many Thousands of Men and Women Have Recovered from Alcoholism, (New York City NY, Alcoholics Anonymous World Services, Inc., 2001), 73.

[46] John Ortberg, The Life You've Always Wanted, (Grand Rapids, MI, Zondervan, 2002),68-69.

[47] Steve Maraboli, Twitter post, 9/15/2016,URL: https://twitter.com/SteveMaraboli/status/776395219373793280

[48] Narcotics Anonymous, 6th ed. (Van Nuys, CA, Narcotics Anonymous World Services, Inc., 2008), 17.

[49] Narcotics Anonymous, 6th ed. (Van Nuys, CA, Narcotics Anonymous World Services, Inc., 2008), 17.

[50] Bill W., Alcoholics Anonymous: The Story of How Many Thousands of Men and Women Have Recovered from Alcoholism, (New York City NY, Alcoholics Anonymous World Services, Inc., 2001), 287.

[51] Bill W., Alcoholics Anonymous: The Story of How Many Thousands of Men and Women Have Recovered from Alcoholism, (New York City NY, Alcoholics Anonymous World Services, Inc., 2001), 45,53.

[52] Bill W., Alcoholics Anonymous: The Story of How Many Thousands of Men and Women Have Recovered from Alcoholism, (New York City NY, Alcoholics Anonymous World Services, Inc., 2001), 64.

[53] Bill W., Alcoholics Anonymous: The Story of How Many Thousands of Men and Women Have Recovered from Alcoholism, (New York City NY, Alcoholics Anonymous World Services, Inc., 2001), 192.

[54] John Ortberg, The Life You've Always Wanted, (Grand Rapids, MI, Zondervan, 2002),132.

[55] Narcotics Anonymous, 6th ed. (Van Nuys, CA, Narcotics Anonymous World Services, Inc., 2008), 94.

[56] Bill W., Alcoholics Anonymous: The Story of How Many Thousands of Men and Women Have Recovered from Alcoholism, (New York City NY, Alcoholics Anonymous World Services, Inc., 2001), 25.

[57] Narcotics Anonymous, 6th ed. (Van Nuys, CA, Narcotics Anonymous World Services, Inc., 2008), 56.

[58] Narcotics Anonymous, 6th ed. (Van Nuys, CA, Narcotics Anonymous World Services, Inc., 2008), 25.

[59] Narcotics Anonymous, 6th ed. (Van Nuys, CA, Narcotics Anonymous World Services, Inc., 2008), 300.

[60] Bill W., Alcoholics Anonymous: The Story of How Many Thousands of Men and Women Have Recovered from Alcoholism, (New York City NY, Alcoholics Anonymous World Services, Inc., 2001), 44-45.

[61] Narcotics Anonymous, 6th ed. (Van Nuys, CA, Narcotics Anonymous World Services, Inc., 2008), 23.

[62] Narcotics Anonymous, 6th ed. (Van Nuys, CA, Narcotics Anonymous World Services, Inc., 2008), 329.

[63] Narcotics Anonymous, 6th ed. (Van Nuys, CA, Narcotics Anonymous World Services, Inc., 2008), 375-76.

[64] Narcotics Anonymous, 6th ed. (Van Nuys, CA, Narcotics Anonymous World Services, Inc., 2008), 52-53.

[65] Narcotics Anonymous, 6th ed. (Van Nuys, CA, Narcotics Anonymous World Services, Inc., 2008), 26.

[66] Narcotics Anonymous, 6th ed. (Van Nuys, CA, Narcotics Anonymous World Services, Inc., 2008), 12.

[67] Narcotics Anonymous, 6th ed. (Van Nuys, CA, Narcotics Anonymous World Services, Inc., 2008), 94.

[68] Narcotics Anonymous, 6th ed. (Van Nuys, CA, Narcotics Anonymous World Services, Inc., 2008), xxvi.

[69] Narcotics Anonymous, 6th ed. (Van Nuys, CA, Narcotics Anonymous World Services, Inc., 2008), 17.

[70] Bill W., Alcoholics Anonymous: The Story of How Many Thousands of Men and Women Have Recovered from Alcoholism, (New York City NY, Alcoholics Anonymous World Services, Inc., 2001), 475.

CPSIA information can be obtained
at www.ICGtesting.com
Printed in the USA
BVHW030414211221
624489BV00001BA/87